...ie world carries deceptive and illusory com-
...onents, and consequently attempt to seek out
... more reliable and permanent grounding
...oint. The monastic recommendation is to
...urn within oneself — always under the proper
...et of guiding principles and nurturing condi-
ions — to rediscover the truer self, which is
...ashioned in the image and likeness of God.
This turn inward leads the self into the presence of fundamental reality. It is to allow this
reality to become greater, more specific, and
more articulate that monastic life is ordered.

The Monastic Impulse is of particular interest to those spiritual seekers who are drawn to
monasticism.

Walter Capps teaches in the religious studies
department of the University of California at
Santa Barbara, was former director of the Hut-
chins Institute, and is the author of numerous
books, including *Religious Personality, Silent
Fire,* and *Vietnam and the American
Conscience.*

THE MONASTIC IMPULSE

THE MONASTIC IMPULSE

WALTER CAPPS

✠

CROSSROAD · NEW YORK

1983

The Crossroad Publishing Company
575 Lexington Avenue
New York, New York 10022

Printed in the United States of America

Library of Congress Cataloging in Publication Data

Capps, Walter H.
The monastic impulse.

Includes bibliographical references.
1. Monasticism and religious orders.   2. Monasteries.
3. Capps, Walter H.   I. Title.
BV4518.C36   1982   255   82-14866
ISBN 0-8245-0490-9

For my brother Roger,
remembering a vow made
early one snow-driven morning
at 49th and Emmett Streets

CONTENTS

1

DISCERNING THE
MONASTIC IMPULSE

The venerable abbot was talking to the student visitors about some of the characteristics of the monastic vocation. He had committed himself to this way of life more than forty years ago. He explained the significance of the daily schedule, the symbolism implicit in the monks' mode of dress, the religious intentions that support the vows of poverty, chastity, and obedience. He described the stages of professional advancement, from novice to full acceptance by the monastic community.

The students were listening intently, taking notes here and there, watching each other, looking for signs of their own reactions. They wanted to know more. They wished to know why one would do it, how it affected the individual. They were intrigued by this vivid demonstration that an entire life could be lived monastically.

One of them asked hesitantly, "Father, if you had it to do over again, would you?"

The abbot heard the question, but it was some time before the answer came.

"Yes, I think so," he said.

But then his demeanor changed. He looked to the group as if asking whether he could dare to share with them what he had come to learn.

He had been born into a family of five brothers, he began. Four of them were still alive, and all of them remained close friends. He said that when he compares his lot with theirs—he was the only one of them to take formal religious vows—he reckons that they have all "come out just about even." He didn't think their ways of life yielded more than his, nor was his calling any more noble than theirs. He repeated that they have all "come out just about even."

Then he paused, stepped back a pace, waiting, as if asking the group if he could go further. He looked out and beyond them, attentive to something more than the immediacy of the situation.

In words carefully selected and barely audible, he continued, "Yes, if I had to do it over again, I would try to change one important component." Again, there was a pause, telling looks to his hearers, and the capturing of a mood that bordered on reverie. "I wish I had been more generous." Having said it, he was completely in place in the room again. He explained.

When he was younger, a student like them, he thought that being critical was an art to be cultivated and most highly prized. This is what his courses of study had led him to conclude. "All of us," he summarized, "have been taught to be critical." It is the art that everyone, sooner or later, learns how to practice. Being critical is the disposition that enables us to find our way. Exercised properly, it is the attitude that makes us well-adapted citizens of the modern world. It gives us access to our place.

Now that he is older, however, he knows that although he might have written five books of criticism of the nation, all of which would have been "devastatingly accurate," and on a subject he knows even more about, the Church, he might have written ten books of criticism, all of which would have been perceptive and substantive, very little distinctive talent would have been required for this. Any of us can do it if we put our minds to it. All that is needed is a careful enunciation of the capacity

modern human beings utilize most naturally and have cultivated most highly.

"Generosity, on the other hand, is a lost art," he continued.
Trained by the dictates of the critical temper, we have lost
touch with generosity. We no longer know what it means, in-
tends, involves. We have only an underdeveloped appreciation
of what it is capable of.

He had become painfully aware that the world is shaped by
the disposition we bring to it. Much of the world of the mid-
twentieth century is a world constructed—no, reconstructed—
by the powers of the critical attitude. He ventured that our
desire to make ourselves feel at home is a telling sign. We have
gotten accustomed to a way of life that, in a number of ways,
runs contrary to our truer natures. We have become so habit-
uated to it that we've even lost sight of the power of the contrast.

Then he smiled. He had wanted to be serious, but he hadn't
intended to become somber. And he hadn't intended to deliver a
sermon. Further, he had even desired to escape being critical.
He wanted to leave the students with a positive word. He had
wished to demonstrate that he felt strong solidarity with them.
He was reaching back, trying to recall the time he was in their
position.

"Generosity is also able to shape the world," he continued.
And then he became more animated as he reflected upon how
life becomes infused with distinctive energies. "Generosity is
also able to shape the world," he repeated, "and is supported to
the fullest by that which abides closest to the center."

This was his message, and he had formulated it in reponse to
the question, "If you had it to do over again, would you?" He
had rediscovered these convictions within himself when he was
invited to tell more of his own story. It was confession before
there was anything of prescription in it. But clearly he was also
speaking for others.

He acknowledged the same in concluding that, when he talks

of generosity in this manner, he is referring to the dynamics of the contemplative life. He explained that for centuries this has been called the *vita contemplativa*. He said it was fostered by the monastic impulse.

The monastic impulse—what is it, and why has it become captivating again? What is the basis of the current revival of interest? Why has interest in monasticism risen to prominence in the contemporary world?

These are questions this book addresses. We are much less interested in statistics on the number of persons entering or leaving monasteries than in coming to terms with the broader appeal of the monastic impulse. And while we are pondering the significance of this current fascination, we must also study the roles that this, the West's most venerable form of counterculture, may be playing in modern society.

My reflections on this subject have been prompted and shaped by a number of visits to monasteries and a growing acquaintance with the sensibilities and values prevalent there. I am not a monk. I have no intention of becoming one. I have only been a visitor, an occasional guest retreatant, and hardly ever for more than a brief period of time—a weekend, part of a week, and, on some occasions, for only a few hours in passing. Yet I have sufficient knowledge that certain aspects of the monastic ideal are immensely appealing and enormously rewarding.

More important, however, is my discovery, as I have journeyed from place to place, that I am not alone in exhibiting interest in the monastic life. Many of the guesthouses of the monastic centers I have visited have been full, and virtually all of them on weekends. Often, one needs to book space weeks and months ahead in order to secure a room. The visitors come from great distances to learn more about the ways in which monks set their priorities and to abide, for a time, in a place where such priorities are honored.

I had known something of these matters before. One cannot

be a student of religion any length of time without encountering the subjects of contemplation, mysticism, and monasticism. The form of first exposure for me—I am recalling the days of my youth—had been deceptive and one-sided. The mystical strain had been presented as contrast religion in dubious or suspicious terms. I had learned of it as a surrogate for a more realistic, this-worldly, incarnational Christian orientation. The incarnational attitude holds the reality of this world to be so necessary and fundamental that any thought of "otherworldly salvation" is simply out of the question. On the other hand, mystical religion exhibits marked otherworldly tendencies. At first appearance, at least, it seems to promote a strategy for releasing oneself from the shackles of the present world. Hence, I was taught to regard it only as a poor substitute, a weak alternative, and, quite probably, an escapist replacement for a truer, more vibrant and responsible way of conducting one's life.

The other way I learned about mysticism was through philosophy courses in school and in the seminary. In the latter, mysticism was treated under the subcategory of epistemology—the science that analyzes how knowledge is acquired—and was presented as an intriguing variation on the prescribed and certifiable methods of knowing. Mysticism was regarded as pertaining to those realms of reality (if there are such) outside the bounds of what the usual methods of knowledge make accessible. Mysticism was linked with extrasensory perception. I was taught that for a host of good reasons philosophers tend to be wary when dealing with such phenomena. They know them to be full of analytical pitfalls and susceptible to exploitation. I was urged, instead, to concentrate on more reliable matters.

Once again, I came away from this abbreviated exposure believing that the mystical way is accessible only to the few who possess the requisite intuitive gifts. Being of precious origin and special derivation, it eluded the impartial and objective means of evaluation. I, therefore, found it exceedingly difficult to reconcile its claims with the more established senses of significance secured by democratic epistemological principles. If one really wanted to be so aloof and elitist, it seemed uncircumspect to be so religiously.

Of course, one can defend religious viewpoints such as the one I knew best by saying that the worthiest goal is to approach the more familiar world with wonder and respect. It is easy to become disconcerted about anyone who finds it necessary to move out of this world to find meaning, or who feels obliged to explore other, more remote regions of human experience to discover the essence of religion. It is apparent that many who undertake such ventures find themselves out of phase with much of the life around them. I didn't wish this to happen to me. Hence, I found a multiplicity of reasons for leaving the matter alone.

The situation did indeed change rather dramatically through exposure to monastic life. No, I have not deceived myself into thinking that the occasional exposure I have had counts for the real thing. And yet I recognized that I had entered a world of intensity, spirit, and intrinsic meaning. It was an encounter for which I had had no proper preparation. I admit to not having taken the life of the monks very seriously before, but more through an attitude of neglect or indifference than overt opposition. Though I knew there were monks in the world, I simply hadn't been paying attention; I knew of no earthly reason why I should. But this also changed after I became acquainted with the writings of Thomas Merton.

I perused Merton's writings first primarily out of a sense of professional responsibility. I recognized that he is part of the contemporary scene in religion, and I regularly offer university courses in this subject area. I was curious about his intentions and accomplishments, and I considered giving him a place in my course syllabus. I thought the students, too, should know who he was; I recognized that his influence is considerable. I didn't approach his writings without bringing some considered expectations. I was particularly intrigued by certain hunches I had about the fate and consequences of the counterculture, and I had come to attach these to my initial interest both in monasticism in general and in Thomas Merton in particular.

Warburg Institute training had persuaded me that cultural phenomena do not simply die or disappear after they have faded from prominence. Rather, they continue to pulsate, perhaps in a subliminal or subterranean form, or they may reappear under a new or revised set of conditions. The powers attributed to the planets in Greek and Roman cosmologies become interiorized eventually, functioning as personal temperaments, habits, psychic realities, and, thus, as the object of interest for psychoanalysis. The figure of the Virgin in medieval iconography is nearly interchangeable later with the figure of Venus, and the transpositions run in the other direction too. Frequently, it has happened that something comes to surface within a culture in advance of its own flowering, then is repressed or becomes submerged, only to reappear again in different guise or in revised form. It has been this way with artistic, literary, and musical forms—indeed, with virtually everything that can be approached as a matter of style or taste. Such occurrences lend force to the probability that the focus of the counterculture of the 1960s was too strong simply to pass from the scene after its initial dramatic dawning. It is more likely, one can conjecture, that portions of counterculture aspirations have been directed (or redirected) toward monastic life, to find new expression there. After all, it is appropriate to interpret monasticism as being the original and most powerful and enduring instance of "counterculture" in the West.

It would follow then that monasticism may be functioning as one of the primary vehicles through which the aspirations of the counterculture are being carried foward, though in much less obvious form. Looked at in another way, it seems plausible that the new interest in monasticism is being fed by some deeper, less obvious currents that have previously made themselves known in other ways. I suspected countercultural origins because of the striking resemblance in intentions. Also, it is perplexing that something so powerful and fruitive as the sixties' counterculture would become so short-lived.

For all of these reasons, I journeyed to the Immaculate Heart Hermitage, also called New Camaldoli, in the Big Sur area of northern California. I chose this destination because of leads provided by William Irwin Thompson in his book, *At The Edge of History*.[1] I wasn't altogether sure what I was looking for. I simply wanted to probe. I didn't know monastic protocol; I had already set something of my own agenda. I recognized that here was a subject about which I should know much more.

Initially, what was most impressive was the eloquent simplicity of the monastic world: the beauty, or esthetic consonance, of its design. It has a fullness, intoxicating as the bouquet of a very fine wine, which in the moment of encounter makes talk about epistemological accountability seem more than a little sterile. I found that I could suspend the resistance I had brought with me.

I believe I became receptive because I could associate the vision with a particular way of life, and not simply with extraordinary human perception. The monastic attitude came to define a specific way of being human, and not simply a special or extravagant way of being either religious or philosophical. Little by little, then more and more, I began to perceive that monasticism places mystical religion within some carefully selected and cultivated nurturing conditions. No longer did it remain in a vacuum, to be abstracted as a psychic reality. Instead, I realized that it is a form of human awareness consonant with a specific way of life. And it carries the prospect that human life need not be forever fabricated and fragmented.

Even when merely visiting, one experiences the release. It was as if many of the tugs and pulls within the more familiar world had been negated, made ineffectual, blocked out by some invisible shield through which one passes along the pilgrimage route to the monastic enclosure. Needs, not wants, become primary, and primary needs become perceptible. Thoughts become transparent. Urges and wishes are vivid. The eye desires to become single again. One is able to listen for the bird song. One notices the detail of a petal of a flower. One finds oneself making resolves to live quietly and simply, not ostentatiously, not to create and confirm impressions of others, but to abide in harmony with all that sustains one fundamentally.

It was this deliberate commitment to simplicity that captured my attention. The monks appeared to be living without extras, luxuries, and excesses. They were disciplined. They appeared to have removed themselves from the temptation to invest in enterprises that merely feed anxieties. I recognized it as a desire to avoid being possessed by one's possessions. It looked like a calculated departure from the lure of the acquisitive spirit.

But their way of life also presented poignant and dramatic contrasts. I knew them to renounce personal possessions, yet it was also apparent that they live in some of the most beautiful and expensive settings on the face of the earth. They confess to making no investments in the fate of the present or current world, yet history certifies that they have been called upon repeatedly to transmit enduring cultural legacies from one generation and era to the next. Similarly, unlike many of their counterparts outside the cloister, they do not cultivate intimate relationships with members of the opposite sex. They practice celibacy, taking the vow of chastity. Yet, from within this stance, they talk almost incessantly above love; and the language they employ is unabashedly lyrical, emotional, passionate, and even erotic. Their lives are made up of a series of contrasts. It must be symbolic, in this regard, that they even alter the daily calendar, turning to sleep while most others are still awake, then rousing themselves in the middle of the night to offer prayers and sing psalms.

They appear to be doing all of it differently. Or, perhaps, because they do it differently, they are not doing it at all. It makes one wonder if they aren't doing something else.

I have found them to be modest when talking about the way of life they are pursuing. I know of no one of them who has said to me that the monastic life is the only way. Nor do they suggest that it is even the better way, or a safer way, or the preferred way. What they emphasize instead is the necessity that there be a contrast, or alternative, to the more prevalent ways. They confess the need to take responsibility for these more prevalent ways too. The monastic way insures that there will be a contrast. In this respect, monasticism functions as a mirror—a mirror that reflects a deep-seated tension.

Yet, while the monastic way maintains the basis for the contrast, it does indeed call provocative attention to the insubstantial character and quality of much of what belongs to the majority attitude. Thomas Merton said that "a monk becomes a completely marginal person to break through the inevitable artificiality of social life." It would be overstating it to say that the monastic attitude reckons the world ("this world") to be evil—that is, all of it evil, without qualification. But monks do find that the world carries deceptive and illusory components. And they know the results can be tragic if one is duped, cajoled, and quietly seduced into trusting the same as a reliable measure of one's enduring worth. They have forceful ways of putting it, all of it meant to illustrate that the way of life promoted in highly sophisticated and complicated civilizations stimulates impulses that run contrary to reality's deepest and truest currents. To take one's cues from "fabricated reality" is to become subject to a succession of disappointments, release from which is possible only through a kind of shock treatment.

The monastic attitude tries to cultivate an alternative. If the world exists in duplicity, then it is important that one seeks out a more reliable and permanent grounding point. The monastic recommendation is that one should turn within oneself, always under the proper set of guiding principles and nurturing conditions, to discover or rediscover the truer self, or, as the monastic literature frequently phrases it, "one's inmost secret center."

Thomas Merton said that life is a question to which the only satisfactory answer is the person. Accordingly, the monastic environment has been established to assist the person "to make the answer audible." Everything about the monastic way of life is designed to assist this process.

Of course, it is customary within the monastic context to talk about God too. And it is through reliable self-discovery that the reality of God is also made known. One turns within the self, understood to have been fashioned in the image and likeness of God, to sense the presence of that fundamental reality Augustine described as "being nearer to us than we are to ourselves." It is to allow that presence to become greater, more specific, and more articulate that monastic life is ordered. It is appropriate, therefore, that monks refer to the general disposition of their way of life as being that of prayer.

This sense of what really matters also helps explain the judicious use of silence within the monasteries. Visitors are often struck by the long pauses that follow the reading of Scripture during the liturgies. Similarly, great discipline is exercised with respect to talking and conversing. Idle talk seems not to be condoned. The same discipline is implicit in the way questions are phrased by the monks. Always they are direct and to the point. Disarmingly direct. Few wasted words. Even fewer conversational fillers. Not much talk about the weather or major-league baseball standings. But neither is all of it serious. It is simply that silence is to be cherished; it is the contemplative's fundamental raw material. When one loses it, the opportunity to penetrate life deeply goes too. Hence it is a treasure one waits for and protects, and it cannot be allowed to become abused.

Solitude, however, does not occur in a vacuum. Rather, the monastic way of life is nurtured by distinctive literary influences. The monk meditates on texts. The silence is punctuated by reading and by listening. The ear is trained to perceive the words that are uttered in silence. Silence is the context, and the word the instrument by which a penetrating, deepening, and stabilizing self-knowledge occurs. Or perhaps it is the other way around: the word is the context, and silence the instrument by which authentic teaching takes place. *Fides ex auditu*—faith comes by hearing. And hearing signifies discerning the words of life that penetrate the silence and inform solitude with character and fullness.

One can learn something about the contemplative impulse by reading the literature the monks have produced. It is very significant, for example, that the writers, for the most part, are cloistered, whether in cells, hermitages, or simply behind monastic walls. Consequently, their writings are marked by definite constraints. Some subjects and territories are simply inappropriate. And what is written is frequently charged with the quality of ultimacy. The temper of the writings is comparable to soliloquy, as though thoughts, feelings and moods are being penetrated, deciphered, and recorded primarily for the benefit of the person to whom they belong. Much of the time, the writer writes for no larger audience than himself. He is recording interior communication. Such communication frequently involves dialogue; but the language is interior. There is no attempt to "communicate out" beyond the experience that is being recorded. Items may be recorded for memory, perhaps because they contain suggestions or insights that require further reflection and elucidation. Thomas Merton's *Asian Journal* consists of notes jotted in his diary. M. Basil Pennington kept a log during his stay on Mount Athos, with no thought of writing it for others; subsequently he was persuaded to have the journal published, and *O Holy Mountain* is the result. Henri Nouwen's *Genesee Diary* has a similar genesis. The historical examples of this tendency are legion.

Hence, to read the mystical literature is nearly to intrude into personal matters, to have a look at something not originally designed for one's eyes. For the most part, the author didn't need an additional reader to complete the sequence of communication. Presumably, the essential completeness was there before the reader arrived or was engaged. It is almost as if the task could have been completed had there been no reader at all. What the reader is given is access to "secrets" from that posture in which self is present to self. Hence, the language both enunciates and conceals. To be sure, at times the secrets are transmitted in the form of encouragement and guidance to others embarked on the same or a similar pilgrimage. But even when this hortatory intention is deliberate, the flavor of the writings is highly individualistic and private.

The literature also reflects an attitude toward life in which there is strong desire for austerity. The monks relinquish privileges in order to be able to devote themselves resolutely to primary needs and obligations. Recognizing that everyone lives and works within restrictions, these persons have taken steps to insure that the limitations are selected ones. They portray it paradoxically, of course, affirming that they find true freedom within their prescribed framework of restrictions. But whatever the effects and interpretations, the fact is that there are myriad facets of human experience into which they choose not to delve. They are exceedingly selective in their appetites. They do not ask to know about everything, and they deliberately resist hearing about some things.

In many important respects, their lives can be likened to that of athletes in training. It is as if they are awaiting a contest that will demand the best they have to give. Hence, they are living under self-imposed discipline, a rigorous regime. Such ascetics recognize that there are pleasures that must be relinquished if one is to be ready and fit when the proper time comes, which hour, as the Scriptures confirm, no one knows in advance.

Such a disposition honors some expectations about what the ongoing course of history will bring. Monastic life is built upon an awareness that life is lived out in the midst of pain and conflict, the resolution of which cannot occur until the conditions of human existence have been transformed. This sense of things gives contemplative literature the character of being emotive, visionary, intensive, and, at times, highly charged. It is a stratum of literature that gives the writer large occasion to express intimate desires and longings.

Appropriately, contemplative experience seems to acknowledge the power of the natural human appetites while purifying—the monks prefer the word *sanctifying*—their content as well as reformulating their intended outcome. In the process, opportunities to satisfy the appetites immediately and directly are sacrificed; and the renunciation is voluntary, given the conviction that the same human desires and longings cannot be gratified until the contradictions and contrarieties in which human life is cast are resolved. The monastic enclosure is the habitat in which the appetites are curbed, the instincts redesigned, the promise of the eventual resolution is taken as a prevailing formative principle, the delays lived out, and the new and fundamental reality is anticipated.

This makes contemplative life resolutely protective of virginal reality. This tendency is made explicit in the reluctance to set the most obvious processes of "generativity" (defined by Erik Erikson as "the concern for establishing and guiding the next generation"[2]) and industry in motion. (In terms of monastic vows, the relinquishment of generativity translates as chastity, the relinquishment of industry as poverty.) Instead there is commitment to an envisioned situation in which all of this can be properly directed and consummated.

From some perspectives, the monastic inclination may look like world denial purely and simply. But the contemplative tends to see it as the most appropriate response one can render while penetrating deeply into the underlying dynamics of things. It is to these dynamics that contemplative life is oriented. In brief, the *vita contemplativa* seeks to enunciate the sense of life that receives creation fresh from the creator's hands, and to abide in this awareness.

It is appropriate, therefore, to receive and mark time with care. To the outsider, such sensitivity is most apparent, perhaps, in the regular tolling of the monastic bells. The bells note the divisions of the day. The saying of divine offices occurs in correspondence with the same discernment. And all of this is indicative of a recognition of differences between the dynamics of the day and of the night, of light and of darkness, of daybreak and of day's end, of dawn and of dusk. Awareness is cultivated, too, of the interdependence of cosmic time with individual time, liturgical time, historical time, as well as cultural time. The motivation is something more than a passion for regularity. The goal is to synchronize the various clocks by which the passage of time is measured. Fundamental to this is the assumption that reality is shaped by synchronous pulsation. Not only does individual life find a greater capacity for growth and development when there is deliberate sensitivity to the passage of time; but the world is made accessible in something closer to its fundamental and primordial depth. Rhythms are important. Cycles pertain. The relations of the stars and planets are closely tied to interior rhythms, patterns, oscillations, and revolutions. The heart of things is beating, and the vibrations and reverberations resound in every place vitality is honored. It is a world that is disclosed in a modified Pythagorean genre, that is, a world marked by the interdependent harmonies of various "musics of the spheres."

The contemporary Nicaraguan poet Ernesto Cardenal, trained under Merton in Gethsemani and, more recently in his homeland, an active supporter and participant in the Sandinista fight against the Somoza regime, presents the religiously revised Pythagorean vision this way:

> All beings share in the same cosmic rhythm. The whirling of the atoms, the circulation of our blood and the sap of plants, the tides of the ocean, the phases of the moon, the circular motion of the stars within their galaxy and the rotation of all the galaxies are all part of the same rhythmic movement, a choral chant sung by the entire cosmos.

Cardenal hears the "music of the spheres" within a variety of concordant melodies.

> ... all the laws of nature are like the strings of a Psalter. The chant of the monks and the cycle of the liturgical year are in accord with the cycle of the harvest, the seasons of the year and the cycle of life and death. And thus the chanting of monks in choir is a participation of the human soul in the rhythms of the sea, of the moon, and the reproduction of animals and stars....
>
> And our song, joined with the choruses of the stars and the atoms, is the same song that is sung by the choir of angels, the same song that is sung perhaps by countless human species and by countless planets ... the joyful shouts of the morning stars which blend with the jubilant voices of the children of God.[3]

I've been present numerous times during postmidnight vigils when the first signs of the new day evoke gratitude, anticipation, and praise. I've sat in choirs alongside monks fresh from early but broken sleep as they've chanted the psalms one after another, always interspersing the chanting with silence, their cadences and candles penetrating the nighttime silence and darkness. I've observed changes in the configuration of the stars, from the beginning of the early-morning office to its close. And I've learned how to distinguish the different sorts of silence that occur in the morning from those at night. I know about the hush that occurs just before daybreak, which even the birds and animals tend to honor, as the deeper night disengages. And I've listened to the stillness that falls at day's end. I've been sensitive to the differences between daylight and nightlight, the differences between night's darkness and day's multivalenced, refracted light. I've watched the world and sky expand as night commences, and I've observed a similar phenomenon when morning breaks. I've learned that some sounds can be heard only when all else has been stilled. And I've come to an increasing and repeated awareness that silence is full of content and infinitely penetrable. I know a little about the closure of silence, not by sound, but by a deeper disengagement, when one's consciousness is brought beyond thought and imagination to some "other room" with its own set of rules over which the subject has no means of persuasion or control.

I've learned from this why, according to the contemplative orientation, the meaning of life doesn't yield to interrogation. It isn't possible or appropriate that everything be thought through. It isn't proper either that the substance of things be "worked out." And surely one is living at cross-purposes when one tries to "figure it out." Rather, the reality to which the monastic attitude is most sensitive is such that it is made accessible only by being engaged. It must be engaged, for it is deemed to be of the same substance or nature as the self. It is a mistake, therefore, to think that the self is trying to establish contact with a reality utterly distinct from itself. Rather, it is a matter of like engaging like. The rhythms of the two entities are meant to coalesce. The pulsations are synchronized. And the resulting unitive act is also understood to be transformative.

In short, monastic life is an attempt to rediscover or recreate the conditions by which life might be engaged in its immediacy, or, as nearly as possible, on its own terms. This intention forms the basis of the outlook with which one must come to terms to understand the intentions of the monastic orientation.

All of it is reflected, I have come to believe, in the eyes. I've looked at monks' eyes. I've studied their eyes. I've been aware of eyes during the long night vigils. I've noticed monks looking at each other, communicating through a highly sophisticated and practiced visual sign language. As I've thought of this, I have recalled the thoughts of Ernesto Cardenal, Elie Wiesel, and Erik and Joan Erikson, all fascinated by the power of eyes.

And, as I've done so, I've pondered the statement in the Talmud, "We do not see things as they are; we see things as we are." Do monks, or contemplatives, see the same world the rest of us do, or are theirs different eyes? Do they see the world via another mode of perception, or is it another world? Can "an eye that is single" penetrate to several dimensions, and find the perceptual basis for allegorical interpretation? That is, does interior silence give formation to its own world, and then such worlds are subsequently seen? I cannot answer such questions, but I suspect that monks' eyes have been tutored in the same way that ears have been trained. They are sensitized to special features. Because human sensibilities are intensified within the monastic setting, the senses of sight and hearing are made more acute.

Along with this special visual and auditory sensitivity is a heightened capacity for detail. I refer to the concern about the esthetic qualities of monastic life, the desire for good order, the compulsions of taste, the gifts that are offered day after day, in countless ways, in praise of beauty. If I hadn't known, I would eventually have recognized that the life of the monastery is dedicated to a wondrously beautiful, alluring yet approachable Lady, one whose presence has inspired the best of which human creative and romantic powers are capable. The reality of "our Lady" is eloquently implicit in monastic life. And the responses to that power, appropriately, are of an adorational nature. The bowing, the deliberate acts of worship and veneration—all of it belongs to the retention of the dictates of courtly love.

A wise and perceptive prior told me once that the way to contemplative reality, at least for men, is through the discovery of the feminine side of their natures. He added that it is because the dynamics of this process of self-discovery are so little known that Westerners have become "psychological pushovers" for advocates of various forms of Asian or Eastern spirituality. The latter claims centuries of practice in enunciating such sensitivities.

The psychologist James Hillman, former director of studies at the Jung Institute in Zurich, suggests in his book *Insearch* that human beings are under psychological compulsion to come to terms effectively with their own masculine and feminine natures. The process involves an identification of a number of interior personages. Hillman calls these "our own inner women, those female images and impulses passing through the corridors of the psyche, often neglected, sometimes cheapened, and certainly misunderstood." He says:

> Since men do live psychologically in a harem, it is useful to get to know one's inner household. We do well to know by what fascination we are bewitched: turned into phallic animal, petrified into immobility, or lured underwater and away from real life. We do well to know whom we are unconsciously following in counsel, where our Cinderella sits in dirt and ashes or Snow White lies in poisoned sleep, what hysterical feminine tricks we play deceivingly on ourselves with effects and moods, which Muse inspires or Beatrice ignites, and which is the true favorite who moves the deepest possibilities of our nature and holds our fate.

The conclusion follows:

> All these women are images of the *anima*, of the soul. Through them is revealed a man's internal life, his personal relationship to himself and to what is beyond himself. Inasmuch as they express my responsiveness and inwardness, they also present forms in which my religious life unfolds. If my soul image is too young, or too cold, or too materialistic, or too critical, then there will be corresponding distortions of my religious life.[4]

Medieval mystics also gave evidence of acknowledging powers and dynamics of this kind. Writing before the era in which psychoanalytic categories had been invented, they expressed themselves in their own idiom. Yet, it is clear that, for them, religious aspiration and the recognition of the presence of the feminine were closely associated. This helps explain why certain female personages become prominent in devotional literature. Dante follows Beatrice as his spiritual guide. The third book *Paradise* of his *Divine Comedy*, is a tribute to her as if—as with Petrarch and Laura—to a great inspiring muse. The Crusaders went under the encouragement of the Queen of Heaven. It was customary for monasteries to be founded as living tributes to the splendor and majesty of our Lady. The entire Cistercian way of life is an eloquent example of these tendencies, for the God adored by Bernard of Clairvaux exhibits both masculine and feminine characteristics, and its feminine aspect is eloquently manifest.

It is also significant, as shall be noted in subsequent chapters, that men and women alike have been able to interpret the outcome of the contemplative process as being like a marriage. That is, both men and women have found ways to depict themselves as "brides of Christ," or "brides of God." It is altogether fitting, too, that the language of nuptial songs should serve as the primary voice of communication. It appears that within such self-consciousness religious and romantic sexual components are so remarkably interdependent that they almost become interchangeable. Hence, it should perhaps not be a cause for alarm that portrayals of mystical experience read as if they are describing erotic experience, and the sexual dimension seems to be ever present within the world of mystical sensitivity.

Saint Augustine was aware of the interpretation of these elements. For example, when responding to the question "And who is God?" he wrote in his *Confessions*:

> . . . what do I love when I love my God? Not material beauty or beauty of a temporal order; not the brilliance of earthly light, so welcome to our eyes; not the sweet melody of harmony and song; not the fragrance of flowers, perfumes, and spices; not manna or honey; not limbs such as the body delights to embrace. It is not these that I love when I love my God.

And yet this indeed is what it is:

> . . . yet when I love him, it is true that I love a light of a certain kind, a voice, a perfume, a food, an embrace; but they

are of the kind that I love in my inner self, when my soul is
bathed in light that is not bound by space; when it listens to
sound that never dies away; when it breathes fragrance that
is not borne away on the wind; when it tastes food that is
never consumed by the eating; when it clings to an embrace
from which it is not severed by fulfillment of desire. This is
what I love when I love my God.[5]

Consequently, it is to be expected that both men and women
have been able to claim Saint Augustine's hymn in praise of
beauty (or, in adoration of God) as drawing upon the language
most appropriate for the occasion. Such heightened sensitivity
to the interpenetration of esthetic, religious, and sexual forces
also comprises the contemporary recovery of the feminine nature of the deity.

The coalescence of these characteristics has led some to suggest that the monastery now stands as a beacon to a recalcitrant
society, a sign that there is a viable alternative to prevailing social, cultural, and spiritual ways. On a broader scale, it is even
conceivable that the monastic impulse may be lending support
to the growing interest in the possibility of designing a fourth
world—which is an orientation to the values of life that is independent of the control of the menacing political conflict between the two superpowers and those who feel obligated to be
in league with either one of them.

These considerations will be taken up in subsequent chapters. For now it suffices to record that one encounters the monastic impulse at New Camaldoli, to the east in Spencer, Massachusetts, further south in Conyers, Georgia, in the heartland
of the nation at New Mellory, Iowa, in Snowmass, Colorado, or
across the ocean in Citeaux, Clairvaux, Maria-Laach, Mont-de-
Cats, Mount Athos, Taizé, and numerous other places. Wherever the monastic impulse has given shape to life, monks can be
found silhouetted against dim light. One can hear the psalms
being chanted, the antiphons flowing gently back and forth between the choirs.

In such a setting, it is easy to become sensitized to the absence of the restrictions of space and time. It is almost as though the individual participants matter far less than the acts they perform, the positions they assume, the postures they exhibit, the attitudes to which they commit themselves, and the thanksgiving they offer in the presence of the mystery they reverence. All this is designed to enunciate an awareness of a deep and abiding reality. Hence, the pulsations in harmony with each other are also coordinant with that by which all things come truly to be—daily, hourly, as the clock ticks, the bells sound, the planets revolve. The earth turns on its axis, day after day, year after year, through centuries and epochs and aeons, as morning follows night and day gives way to evening, like the waves moving toward the shore and then receding along the coastline. Life continues as it has for centuries. It is conceivable that there is no time during the day or night, no moment in the world's daily existence, when there isn't a monk somewhere keeping a lonely vigil, bowing fully and deeply before an altar. At all times, around the clock and around the world, there exists persistent and perpetual awareness of the resourcefulness of the *vita contemplativa*. And the prospect is that, had there been no mystical, contemplative or monastic religion, the other forms of religion may not have survived into the modern world. Take it away and something close to the heart of religious sensitivity goes with it.

2

THE MERTON LEGACY

Certainly no one could have known in December 1968, when Thomas Merton died in Bangkok, Thailand, that the next few years would see the arrival of a new contemplative era in religion, and that Merton's life and thought would be one of its primary forces.

December 1968 was a time of transition. It was a period of profound political upheaval, social and cultural adjustment, and institutional change. The Vietnam War was becoming a burden, embarrassment, and incontrovertible tragedy. The student protest movement had gathered momentum. The counterculture was in full dress. The Johnson administration was giving way to the reascendency of Richard Nixon, who, in turn, was issuing manifestos regarding his aspirations for his first term of presidential office. In the electoral process immediately preceding, the country had become well acquainted with Eugene McCarthy, Robert Kennedy, Hubert Humphrey, Nelson Rockefeller, and Chicago's Mayor Daley. It had been years before, on January 29, 1961, that President John F. Kennedy had declared to the nation and to the world that "the torch has been passed to a new generation of Americans" who are "willing to pay any price, bear any burden, to assure the survival and the success of liberty." A half decade had passed since President Kennedy had been assassinated. Six months had passed since the murder of his brother, and more than eight months since the killing of Martin Luther King, Jr. The nation was in a state of prolonged shock. There was turmoil, confusion, but no absence of large resolve. Looking back, the novelist Peter Tauber refers to 1968 as a singularly important year, "an extraordinary moment in the world's life, another in the periodic high tides in the culture and politics of men," a year when "revolution was itself the natural order, when politics and culture combined and altered each other."[1] It was the year when the new leftists joined forces to form the National Mobilization Committee to End the War in Vietnam, the year when General Curtis E. LeMay, former Air Force chief of staff, and then vice-presidential running mate of George Wallace, said that he "would use anything that we could dream up, including nuclear weapons, if it was necessary to win the war." It was also the year of the Poor People's Campaign, and the creation of Resurrection City on the mall in the nation's capital. All of this was before Watergate. It was well ahead of the Kissinger era of foreign diplomacy. Spiro Agnew wasn't yet a household name. Jimmy Carter hadn't yet become governor of Georgia. Charles de Gaulle was still alive.

In religious circles, the vogue was the revised "social gospel." There was much emphasis upon the need to establish the kingdom of God on earth. Yes, it almost seemed as if the kingdom of God had become the theological equivalent of the Great Society. The Protestant world rallied behind the slogan of the World Council of Churches assembly in Uppsala, Sweden: "Behold, I make all things new." The Catholic world was living in the aftermath of the Second Vatican Council. The shift from dogma to experimentation, from permanence to change, was growing in influence. And in the churches, baroque organ music was being replaced by a laid-back, syncopated beat, fashioned to the sound of Spanish guitars. In large numbers, priests and nuns—sometimes together—were leaving the orders and seeking release from their vows. Religious houses, churches, and monasteries were being vacated, and religious institutions were being severely challenged. Hans Küng was not the only theologian who exhorted his readers and hearers to "support the unrest wherever you find it." It was a time of transition.

Some of the best song lyrics of the time, and of the movement, were provided by Bob Dylan, Paul Simon, and John Lennon and Paul McCartney. The Beatles had just released "Hey Jude." Peter, Paul, and Mary, favorites of many years, were still singing and performing together, but Mary had announced that she was "leaving on a jet plane; don't know when I'll be back again." In the midst of this, Joan Baez, with her soft voice, sparkling white teeth, and deep moral sensitivity, returned again and again to Sproul Plaza in Berkeley to lend beauty and direction to the movement. But, strangely enough, it was Burt Bacharach who raised the question sung about most often: "Do you know the way to San Jose?"—all about "parking cars and pumping gas," as if the most obvious, ordinary places were becoming difficult to find.

It was December 1968, and the safer, surer, more majestic, and predictable worlds of Karl Barth, Paul Tillich, Reinhold Niebuhr, Karl Rahner, and Jacques Maritain seemed to have passed from the scene. They had been brought down by the effects of dramatic change. Such change was in keeping with the power of the critical temper to call all things into question. Everywhere, from every quarter, there was something new "blowing in the wind," as Bob Dylan put it.

In December 1968, on a gentle hillside, a short distance from the walls of the chapel of Gethsemani Abbey, near Louisville, Kentucky, a community of Trappist monks gathered to lay the body of Thomas Merton ("Father Louis," as they called him) to rest. He had lived in the abbey for twenty-seven years, having come there from New York City and the English literature department of Columbia University. In Gethsemani, he had lived the life of the monk, adhering to the obligations, the vows and responsibilities within the monastic walls. Within the same walls, he had written all but the first few of his many books and articles. He was a monk who was a writer, a writer who was a monk. His literary habitat was the cloister. From that vantage point, he looked out on the world—the "other world"—and interpreted the events of the day through religious and human sensitivities and by means of literary skills fashioned in the cell.

Only a few months prior to this memorable day in December 1968, Merton had gone to Asia to participate in a number of conferences on religious renewal. He went there to learn from the Asian monks, because in these matters, as he had said, they were far ahead of their counterparts in the Western world. As he had left the airport in San Francisco, he had written in his diary: "I am going home, to the home where I have never been in this body." He referred to "being at last on my true way after years of waiting and wondering and fooling around." Then he had prayed, "May I not come back without having settled the great affair."[2]

Before leaving the States, he had gone to the Center for the Study of Democratic Institutions in Santa Barbara, where he gave a brief talk on the theme "the monk as marginal man." Here he identified with those on the edges of society—poets, students, "hippies," as he called them—who were raising critical questions. He also spoke of the need to develop a "universal consciousness," adding that "we are not going to solve the social problems of community unless we solve them in universal terms." Then, after spending some days in retreat in Redwoods Monastery in northern California, he had gone on to India, Tibet, Sri Lanka, and Thailand. There he lectured, visited monastic centers, conducted interviews with Asian religious leaders and spiritual masters, and participated in conferences. And, in Bangkok, on December 10, following an address in which he elaborated upon the remarks he had made at the Center earlier in the fall, Merton was accidentally electrocuted. His body was returned to the States by an American army plane from Vietnam. The funeral service was held at the abbey on December 17, 1968.

Something of the significance of Merton's life was recognized immediately. More than any other individual, he was responsible for giving Christian monasticism a revised and updated reason for being. He understood how this "alternative way of life" could be expressed in terms of the explicit needs and demands of the modern world. He developed a monastic point of view that was in correspondence with the dynamics of social change. And he did so in keen awareness of the practical implications of prevailing political orientations. Even from within the walls of the cloister, he was in close touch with the revolutionary movements of the sixties.

Much was known about Thomas Merton in 1968. He had gained a large readership ever since the publication, in 1948, of his autobiographical book *The Seven Storey Mountain*. His subsequent books were widely circulated. Many people had gotten accustomed to looking to him for guidance regarding ways in which religious sensitivity might become congruent with other necessary obligations.

But what was not known, and could not have been known, is the remarkable complementarity between Merton's interests and many of the important tendencies in the religious climate that has come into prominence since his death. For this period of time has been characterized by an impressive turn to contemplative religion, and a growing preoccupation with its dictates. We can properly refer to the development as the dawning of the contemplative era. Before this occurred, a more dominant tendency was to construe religion, in the main, as a sociopolitical force, to look to it as a transforming and regenerative power within a society experiencing profound social and political change. The new era, by contrast, has called for a renewal of the classic spiritual disciplines, including prayer and meditation. In the process, the rediscovery of contemplative religion has helped identify a genre or mode of experience so complete and resilient that it had been utilized as the spectrum through which life itself is approached and addressed.

The shift was dramatic, and involved a complete turnabout. In its wake, it was not as much the God above, or even the God ahead, but the God within who was sought and worshipped. It was not as much faith, or hope, but love that served as the fundamental motivating force. It was not so much the establishment of the ideal society on earth that stood as chief objective, but the cultivation of "interior space," or, more specifically, an awareness of the reciprocal harmonies between the soul's (or the deepest self's) pulsations and natural and cosmic rhythms. No longer a world in which large place was made for devotees of "the social gospel," the new era was marked by the return of the Pythagorean genre, with its bold perceptual sensitivity to "the music of the spheres."

Lest we extend these distinctions into misleading radical contrasts, we should keep in mind that Merton understood contemplative life to be an instrument of social reform. It is evident, too, that he refused to approach *action* and *contemplation* as competing forces. He recognized that there are large areas of overlap, subtle similarities, and a persistent and necessary complementarity. In his view, contemplation finds expression in action, and action is always fed, directed, and enriched by contemplation. But action also finds expression in contemplation. Hence, while it makes obvious sense to talk of "contemplation in a world of action," one can also speak appropriately of action within a more comprehensive world of contemplation. The two dispositions always belongs together. Each gives form to a world in which the other is a necessary component.

Part of the reason the new contemplative era came on with such force is Merton's own catalytic influence. It is clear that he didn't look upon himself as a religious reformer or a social revolutionary. Ever since he took the vows recorded in *The Seven Storey Mountain*, to live his life in the Cistercian abbey in Kentucky as "one of the poor men who labor in Gethsemani," he desired simply to be a monk. This was his fundamental intention. And he was consistent. The end of his life found him seeking an even greater monastic quiet and solitariness than he had known before. He had thoughts about moving to Alaska, for example, and was wondering about establishing something more remote at or near Redwoods Monastery in northern California. But never did he display any interest in making more of monasticism than it was. He was not inclined to promote anything, to create new programs and institutions, to link the monastic way to specific sociopolitical causes. He was not a campaigner. He would have been repulsed by many of the temptations implicit in monastic religion's sudden and dramatic currency. But this is not to suggest that he was indifferent. For he worked diligently from within the monastery for changes and updating. He was encouraged both by his abbot and community and by the Vatican to engage in these efforts as well as to interpret the monastic form of religious life to persons outside the cloisters. He was obliged, for religious and vocational reasons, to write, then to write again, and to write some more. Some say that he wrote too much. Even he said that he wrote too much, and he remained displeased with much that he wrote. In spite of this, he always found interested readers and commentators, and their number has increased since his death. His autobiographical reflections and interpretive work generated keen and growing interest. His efforts to modify and update monastic life from within found large visibility, acceptance, and a more extensive application.

Even today, we may be too close to the situation to comprehend how it happened. Without anyone's intending or seeking it, efforts designed simply to revivify the monastery from within were transmitted beyond and were transposed into the basis for a dramatic, more pervasive change in religious attitudes and human aspirations. How did it happen that a religious viewpoint, very monastic in temper and substance, found a larger, more inclusive basis of resonance? And even if we could explain and trace the connections, we would still find the changes to be dramatic.

Looked at in this way, the situation contains some of the characteristics necessary to evoke Erik Erikson's interpretive category "cultural work." Erikson understands cultural work to occur when a previous prevailing way of looking at the world is subjected to critical assessment, then either requires revision or replacement by a viewpoint more resilient and compellling. Until the reconstructive work is effected, persons living in an era cannot find the language or the terminology to realize appropriate connectedness. In seeking a basis for understanding himself and his place both in society and history, the "cultural worker" functions in a representative capacity. Others come to accept the correspondence he reconstructs and the resonances he reestablishes. Thus, his activities as a person of uncommon intuitive sensitivity and creative ability assume more extensive collective acceptance and sociocultural application.[3]

Thomas Merton qualifies as a cultural worker because he was engaged in this primary reconstructive work. In seeking to effect monastic reform from within (so the analysis would have it), he tapped into certain ideological dynamics that carried a larger range of application. That is, he helped mark out an orientation to life with which others could identify. They, in turn, came to regard him as leader, guide, and pioneer in an effort in which they too were engaged, even if unwittingly. For himself, and on their behalves, he worked to bring the new situation into focus and intelligibility. He helped make the new genre perceptible. Through his writings, influences, and intentions, it was given delineation, perhaps most of all because, as with Saint Augustine, the interpretive and constructive work was expressed through autobiographical portrayals. It isn't simply that he recognized the new circumstance when it came to pass—he helped bring it to pass. Indeed, the personal moves he made— both subjectively and from behind the walls of the cloister, including the journey to Asia—found large spheres of influence. It was a matter of the time being ready for the insights of the individual, and of the individual having known and probed enough to be able to meet the demands of the time. Consequently, the developments since Merton's death are rightly perceived as extensions of his life. And the shifts in religious awareness with which he can be associated can be seen to coalesce with a larger trend, a shift of direction within the society.

The new orientation assumed ascendency in the following manner. During a time of great collective enthusiasm and self-confidence, in the early and mid-sixties, human aspirations were joined to a series of well-intended social, economic, and political reforms. Their products were most impressive; indeed, they inspired a veritable revolution in our sense of common destiny and corporate potential. Yet, no matter how impressive and engaging, the reforms were also disappointing, or, at least, the enthusiasms wedded to them could not find full satisfaction. Perhaps the intended changes were too numerous. Perhaps the intentions were overly ambitious. Perhaps it was unrealistic to expect that all could be changed at once. Perhaps the process broke down at the point of implementation. Perhaps there was insufficient political will. Maybe the resistance was greater than the force for change.

For whatever reasons, in the general collective malaise that followed there developed an increasing lack of confidence in programs, and particularly in those that come under the sponsorship of "bureaucrats." As an alternative, persons have come more and more to rely upon their own individual resources and inventiveness, and to expect others to do the same. The shift can be seen across the land, and it affects politics, economic incentives, patterns of development and growth, and, not least, the ways in which citizens of the United States relate to other peoples and other nations. It was to be expected, then, that the same shift would be reflected in the nation's religious habits. Religion, too, became more individualistic and introspective, more spiritual and contemplative, and, correspondingly, less socially minded and less politically active.

It would be inaccurate, however, to portray the transition in simple contrasting terms. For while the shift worked to deemphasize some religious aspirations that had been prominent before, it also served to bring some others to new and vigorous attention. With the coming of the contemplative era came a strong and renewed respect for the earth, and, beyond it, for the cosmos. Emphasis was directed toward disciplining one's patterns of daily exercise and eating habits. New attention was given to cherishing and safeguarding times of silence. And with these came heightened sensitivity to the various harmonies by which human life can be principled; increased awareness of the negative and debilitating effects of aggression; the serious casting about for models of life independent of the familiar success syndrome; the growing awareness that GNP (gross national product), though an accurate economic indicator, cannot measure degrees of satisfaction lying beyond its grasp; the craving for enduring health; the desire to live more simply, indeed, the insistence on simplifying human need. All of this is a part of the tendency we are chronicling. We can summarize the development by referring to it as the birth of a *new asceticism*.

Thomas Merton was not alone in sensing its birth. E. F. Schumacher found access to a portion of it, too, in his book *Small Is Beautiful*, in which the encouragement of economic reforms was presented as a means of revising human incentives more comprehensively. And, as the discussion Schumacher sparked went forward, it became apparent that "small is beautiful" focused attention on quantities of scale as a lead-in to a more crucial topic: the observation that when life is addressed in an instrumentalist way—when most things are done to advance oneself or to promote a cause—one's connections with reality become badly skewed. Eventually, "small is beautiful" came to symbolize diminished confidence in the proposition that human needs are met effectively when programs are devised, projects are conceived, and proposals are generated.[4]

That is, it wasn't simply a change in mood. It also involved the altering of fundamental aspirations. Confidence reached out for more reliable means of support. Basic assumptions about how life ought to be lived were questioned. Uncertainties about how collective goals were to be defined became deeper and more pervasive. More and more people came to sense that the methods that had been utilized to bring humankind to this stage in its development were probably not the ones that could carry it further. Thus, there was a reaching out for something more, or something additional, or something different.

Stephen Graubard, editor of *Daedalus*, explained portions of the collective anxiety and the shift in the following way in introducing a special issue of his journal:

> Americans, in the late nineteen-fifties and early nineteen-sixties, were not disinclined to boast of their scholarly achievements . . . . The country's aptitude for spectacular invention had in no way diminished; the explorations in space and the flight to the moon gave evidence of this. For those who valued more theoretical scientific capabilities, America's record seemed no less spectacular.

But then something happened:

> It is difficult to know when the first shocks to this excessive pride were recorded. Some will argue for Berkeley in 1965, where the dubiety of students about the exaggerated claims of professors was first registered. Others will see the development of criticism in more global terms . . . . Institutions that had not previously been subjected to persistent public scrutiny—at least not to hostile scrutiny—discovered that claiming a worthy purpose was no longer a sufficient defense. A larger vindication of past conduct was demanded. Some were frightened that certain of these institutions might not be able to survive the attacks; others, more sanguine, imagined that the tumult and the disorder might, in the end, have a cleansing effect.[5]

Graubard was not alone in recognizing that the exercising of the critical temper had been extended to virtually every corner and level of society. Every institution was subjected to analysis, criticism, and the need for redefinition. The courts, the schools (at all educational levels), religious institutions, the business community, industry, government—indeed, the components of the entire social-institutional fabric—were submitted to the most comprehensive critical assessment that any society has yet undergone. Thus, there were times when the democratic state found itself in a situation of vast confusion and disarray, unsure of its direction, not lucidly and confidently able to identify and define its values, persisting in a void created by the dissolution and abolition of a vital, shared sense of life. Henry Steele Commager was not the only one to ask, "What has become of the American dream?" Morris Dickstein, in *Gates of Eden*, published in 1976, observed that "the *idea* of America, the cherished myth of America," is the victim of a "shattering blow."

Henry Aaron of the Brookings Institution offered an intriguing explanation of what had happened. In his book *Politics and the Professors*, Aaron suggested that it was *critical analysis* that did it all in. It was an overextension of the problem-solving mentality. He wrote:

> The role that research and experimentation played in the demise of the simple faiths of the early nineteen-sixties was not accidental. The process by which research and experimentation is created corrodes the kind of simple faiths on which political movements are built; this effect is particularly strong when, as in the late nineteen-sixties and early nineteen-seventies, the actions of political leaders tend to destroy those faiths, and events make them implausible.

He added:

> This corrosive role of research and experimentation was obscured for a while because nearly all of it was produced by analysts who themselves held the simple faiths that underlay the goals of the Great Society.[6]

But, before long, according to Aaron, "the imperatives of the analytical process won out." In the end, critical analysis showed itself to be "an intellectually conservative force" within the society. Hence, the struggle reached much deeper than the level of the persistent clash between liberal and conservative forces. Rather, in Aaron's view, the intellectual consensus upon which collective aspirations depend simply collapsed.

Yale historian George W. Pierson, reflecting on the ways in which learning affects public policy, tended to agree. He offered that perhaps the problem-solving orientation had been overused. He generalized:

> We Americans have a problem with problems and issues. We overdo them. We're addicted to problems: they've become a cultural habit. Anything and everything that bothers us we try to formulate into a problem, then we go to work on it and solve it. All problems in the American definition . . . are solvable. So we keep hoping that even the greatest issues can be resolved if only they can be stated and studied.

Pierson referred to this expectation as a kind of "drug habit," calling it an "addiction to problem-solving." "What I am trying to suggest," he wrote, "is that not all evils or controversies or public discomforts can be shaped into problems; not all novelties are excellent, and not all issues are real." To repeat, "We should recognize that not all difficulties are problems, and not all problems are solvable, and not all issues are urgent, or even issues at all."[7]

John Gardner, founder of Common Cause in 1970, issued a new book in 1978, *Morale*, in which he deplored the loss of a compelling collective vision. "When a society disintegrates," he wrote, "you may be sure that its animating ideas and ideals died first in the minds of men and women." Gardner believed it essential that there be a new vision, a sense of shared values, a "dream of a greatness to come." Acknowledging this shift in the direction of his enthusiasms, Gardner described the new task as follows:

> My life for the past dozen years has been wholly devoted to action and conflict in the political and social arena, and to practical work on concrete issues—from the improvement of education to the reform of election campaign financing. I have been wholly preoccupied with specific solutions to specific problems.
>
> Now I want to step back and look at the motives that underlie social and political action. . . . From an active life in the public arena, I know all too well the case for cynicism and surrender. But there are things to be said. . . . It is especially important now for us to realize that just as shared beliefs and values are susceptible to decay, so are they capable of regeneration. The processes of decay are always at work, but so are the regenerative processes.[8]

William de Bary, identifying the same spirit, observed that "young people [now] feel a powerful urge to affirm and not just to criticize."[9] To affirm, and not just to criticize—but this requires the capturing of a new orientation.

Within the more specifically religious world, the shift was reflected in fine books like John Dunne's *The Reasons of the Heart*, published in 1979, and Henri Nouwen's splendid *The Way of the Heart*, published in 1981. Emphasis lay upon heart, rather than mind or criticism or the powers of analytical mind. Dunne's book carried the subtitle "A Journey into Solitude and Back Again into the Human Circle." Like the temper from which it derives its life, it is a plea for gentleness. It solicits a more delicate mediation based on the nature of things, in contrast to rigorous analytical probing. And it can also be read as a quest for a lost, disguised, richer but less formal and rigid basis of human authority.

The realignments Dunne advocated could be found in scores of other books. Indeed, bookstores became filled with them—

new treatises on "spirituality," new translations and reissues of classical mystical writings, guidebooks on spiritual formation, manuals of prayer and meditation, pamphlets on spiritual direction, and the like. Retreat centers—in contrast to the situation in the mid-sixties—were full again. People who wanted to go there found that their names were placed on waiting lists. And, as this was happening, a number of colleges and universities created new programs in contemplative studies. Some even took steps to establish research centers in the field. All of this was taken by many advocates of the movement to signify the birth of a new era in human awareness, or, if not that, at least a time of significant religious revival.

The cross-cultural fallout was impressive too. The monasteries in the West had been affected by Asian religious influences, and this altered their own sense of identity and purpose, not to mention their worship practices. East was meeting West, and West was meeting East. But this time through, the lines of cultural transmission became extraordinarily complex: in the meeting of East and West, the West learned to face itself in a new way, that is, from the East. And while this was occurring within Christian monasteries, the monastic centers of the Asian world were being transplanted to the United States. The monks themselves embarked upon the very complicated task of sorting out significant cross-cultural currents. They functioned, as in days of old, as ministers of cultural and religious exchange. That is, they brought the riches of one culture into rapprochement with others, and in the meeting discovered new and refreshing insights. Hence, what they attempted to effect religiously and spiritually carried profound social and cultural ramifications.

The theological ramifications are significant too. For example, the more dogmatic theological traditions within Christianity tend to present God as a parent, usually as the Father (but increasingly as both father and mother), as in "Our Father who art in heaven." This formulation is retained, of course, within the contemplative revival. After all, Saint Augustine is not the only classical Christian theologian who named the deity "the one who made us," and we, in turn, "his offspring." But it became increasingly apparent that this way of conceiving things places God in the position of being an authority figure, in the main, and construes religion as being a matter of obedience to His commands and will. This is the way it should be; the tradition contains strong support and compelling arguments for it. And yet, in the combination of these ingredients lies the basis for the charge that religion functions as an instrument of enslavement. Authoritarian religion always functions to keep some persons in bondage, subject to exploitation by demands they may never fully understand. Under such terms, believers live their lives under the will and rule of an overarching parental figure who is simultaneously feared, worshipped, and adored. And they find it difficult to look upon themselves as being anything other than children.

The recovery of the contemplative tradition allowed an alternative to surface. For in spite of the fact that the monastic vision sustains a strong sense of "otherworldliness" and vests power and authority in a transcendent deity (properly conceived as a parent), it also teaches its advocates to discern the presence of God within oneself and to become sensitive to the dictates of the human heart. Hence, there lies within contemplative literature the theological possibility of finding connectedness with God to be more a matter of fidelity and espousal than of law and obedience. The authority that is nurtured is like an inner compulsion. Thus, although it is always appropriate for the believer to view himself as a child who is known under the watchful eye of a heavenly parent, it is also appropriate for him to view himself as having been invited to share in the love of one to which he has been espoused. And the literary legacy for this within the Christian contemplative tradition is the Song of Songs— the primary textual carrier of the mystical tendency within the Christian religion.

The contemplative revival made such theological revisions possible and attractive. And, in a more comprehensive sense, it assisted persons who were searching for ways to redefine and realign human enthusiasms and expectations. For the monastic attitude was recognized to be congruent with the craving for simplicity, the deep desire to recapture what is fundamental in life, to overcome the instrumentalist tendency by returning to a more natural setting. One finds this expressed in concern for the care of the environment, in ecological sensitivities, in the pursuit of alternative forms and sources of energy, in the collective alarm regarding contamination, pollution, spoilation, indeed, the organized opposition to artificiality and fabrication of all sorts and varieties. The same may be interpreted as signs of recognition that some of the features of the technological society and the technocratic age carry heavy debilitating consequences. It indicates, too, that prevailing ways of measuring personal success and failure have become grossly deceptive, and that human beings recognize themselves to have become motivated by causes and instincts that are manifestly ephemeral. The monastic alternative holds out the prospect that human life can be put on a more fundamental basis. And, within the past years, that way of life has become more available to persons who have sensed that humankind's most prominent ways of addressing reality seem discordant with the way reality is fundamentally ordered.

Naturally, persons so affected welcomed these developments as being among the most positive humanly achievable. The same occurrences helped qualify Thomas Merton as the symbol of the movement. His life and thought were identified with the dawning of the new era. He also was recognized as having marked out the contours of the new world while preparing pathways for others to follow.

This in brief was how it happened. Yet it is not a simple matter to judge. Although many greeted the new era with accolades, just as many were profoundly worried. After all, to acknowledge that problem-solving techniques have been proven to be incomplete and unsatisfactory does not necessarily lend success and satisfaction to whatever is there to fill the vacuum. And to recognize that collective aspirations are no longer easily supported by "dreams of greatness" does not necessarily mean that credence should be given to whatever one does to try to restore one's confidence. It may very well be that the turn to contemplative religion should be viewed as being more symptomatic of the larger plight than an adequate response. It may indeed provide its adherents with a way of living in the absence of more effective ways of coming to terms with the world. But this may simply mean that it is an effective and religiously sanctionable way of withdrawing, more or less, from critical involvement in more centrist sociocultural and political enactments. In other words, to become contemplative may mean finding safe harbor, or a resting place, at the margins or in a counterposition some distance away from the demands of the immediate fray. From this perspective, the adoption of the contemplative attitude may signal a profound loss of nerve, a calculated antidote to some early overextensions or overcommitments, and some basic indolence, apathy, or even a preference for purely personal preoccupations.

This is how Christopher Lasch would see it, following the analysis in his brilliant book *The Culture of Narcissism*. Referring to the prevailing life interests of many persons living in the aftermath of the Vietnam War, and the disappointments of the sixties, Lasch observes: "Having no hope of improving their lives in any of the ways that matter [by which he means collective social and political ways, of course], people have convinced themselves that what matters is psychic self-improvement." Lasch knows what this signifies. "Harmless in themselves," he continues, "these pursuits, elevated to a program and wrapped in the rhetoric of authenticity and awareness, signify a retreat from politics and a repudiation of the recent past."[10]

This is the way others, through the centuries, have seen it

too. The Protestant reformer Martin Luther, after leaving the Augustinian order, had some harsh things to say about the monastic way of life. In his 1521 essay *"De votis monasticis"* Luther called the monastic way a "form of bondage." The year before, in his famous tract "The Babylonian Captivity of the Churches," he charged monasticism with being "more hostile to faith than anything else can be." Luther believed the monks to be excessively preoccupied with themselves, and, in that state, highly susceptible to the temptations of "pride and presumption." Instead of busying oneself with one's soul and spiritual progress, Luther counseled the followers of Christ to "serve the well-being of others."

Part or our task is to come to terms with such assessments, that is, to judge the contemporary contemplative revival according to such standard and perennial attitudes. We shall approach the subject by encouraging the monastic impulse, as it were, to manifest itself on its own terms. We will take our inquiry inside the monasteries themselves. In keeping with Merton's own vocational affiliation, we shall be traversing a Cistercian pilgrimage route primarily, knocking on doors of Trappist abbeys. Regardless of the specifics of our final assessment, one essential fact prevails: in the years following Thomas Merton's death, what had been relegated to the margins of social and cultural life has moved much closer to the center.

3

GETHSEMANI

G ethsemani Abbey in Kentucky is nearly as well known as Thomas Merton. Gethsemani had been Merton's home for twenty-seven years. He left for the Orient in 1968, on the famous pilgrimage from which he never returned. Gethsemani was the abbey to which Merton had come when, as a retreatant back in 1941, he arrived from Columbia University in New York City. He had sought out this place prior to deciding to become a monk. Then he stayed. Many of the men who had lived with him daily, the Trappist fathers and brothers, are still there. He made a deep impression not only upon them but also upon the entire Trappist community, and far beyond monastic life itself through the influence of his numerous and regular publications.

"Gethsemani Abbey near Louisville, Kentucky," the description one encounters so often in Merton literature, is imprecise. The monastery is approximately an hour's drive south from Louisville. On the way, one can find few people who are able to help with directions. Many more know how to get to Abraham Lincoln's birthplace nearby. I had come into the territory on a cold, blustery winter's day in mid-December.

I knocked on the door of an entrance that had been placed to the left of what appeared to be the doors that were opened on Sundays or regular feast days or when large groups of people were moving in or out. After a moment or two, a very correct, neat, circumspect-looking monk opened the door and welcomed us inside. I explained who I was, how far I had come, why I had chosen to take a detour on my way home in order to visit Gethsemani.

I was urged to go inside. To distinguish myself from the host of travelers, retreatants, and tourists who come to Gethsemani, I invoked my professional credentials, modestly, of course. I said to the monk that I had read many of Thomas Merton's books. What is more, I went on, I had become personally acquainted with a few Trappist monks. I mentioned their names, speaking the words slowly, hoping to expand the rapport being established. I referred again to the itinerary I had been following, and assured our hearer, whoever he was, that I intended to stay only a brief time. I also told him that I had but one specific request, that I might speak briefly with Brother Patrick Hart, Merton's secretary. The person to whom I had been addressing these orientational remarks extended his hand once again to shake mine. He said simply, "I am Patrick Hart"—the man I most wanted to see.

We talked for nearly an hour. Merton's writings had prompted many questions. But I was even more curious about the personal dimensions of the man. What was Thomas Merton really like? I mean, as an individual, on a day in–day out basis? What can be said about his personal temperament, his sense of his own significance? Did he ever give anyone a chance to know him well? I wondered if the Thomas Merton who is accessible through books is the same Thomas Merton the monks knew, or if there was another that few had an opportunity to become acquainted with.

And what about his awareness of the role he was playing? Had he any realistic sense of his own influence? Was such influence deliberate on his part? And, if it were, how did he square all of this with the attitude of withdrawal and disengagement that he had counseled to others? Wasn't he himself involved in calculatedly constructive cultural work? And what about correspondences and/or conflicts between his work outside and his standing inside the monastery? How did other members of the community relate to him? What did they think of him? Was he accorded special privileges because of his notoriety? Was it apparent even to them that he was unusually gifted, or was this reputation based primarily on the reception of his books by those outside the monastery?

I also wondered what Merton may have been moving toward before he died. I wanted to know about thresholds he may have been standing upon and wanted to cross. Was Merton really intending to go somewhere else? Was he planning to survey Alaska, or some part of California, as legend holds, wishing to establish a monastery elsewhere almost outside of public and human reach? Was he considering moving his contemplative home to a place not regulated by the confines of Western culture? Had he considered abandoning his vows? Was he thinking of leaving the cloister or of radically modifying monastic life?

Then, too, I was thinking about the rash of puzzling, enigmatic, but probably brilliant passages in the *Asian Journal*, the last words and sentences he set to paper. How much importance had he attached to his trip to Asia? In what sense was it symbolic of certain interior moves he was also in the process of making? What did he mean when he wrote that the ground he was covering by foot he had already traversed in his soul? What, specifically, did he expect to learn from the Asian monks, those monks of non-Christian orientation? Was it an extension of his own interests, calculated augmentation, the quest for something new and different, or simply a desire for greater skillfulness in contemplative techniques? Why had he become so interested?

His fascination with Marxist political ideology also left me wondering. So too his identification with certain student groups that were calling for dramatic and thorough social and political change, his prompt and genuine association with some of the earliest forms of the counterculture. I was perplexed and intrigued by the combination of these various interests. What did it all mean to him? Did he believe, for example, that the world was undergoing an epochal transition, a cataclysmic change, passing to another era and stage in its development? Had he lived, would he have wanted to adopt the mantle of the prophet, calling his hearers to both intense self-reflection and penance? How would he have responded to the strong and intense emotional demands of the prolonged Vietnam era? Did he truly sense the pulsations of a society and culture in the process of transformation? Was there anything of the Teilhardian expectation in him? Was his journey to Asian countries an attempt to fit himself for the age on which humanity was about to embark? Were his sensibilities so marked? Or could it have been that his exposure to Asian forms of meditation had carried him beyond Christianity itself? Was he interested in a post-Christian, indeed, posttraditional form of religious orientation? Was he attempting to search out the components of a new style of religious agreement? Religious complementarity? The basis of a new synthesis? Did Patrick Hart know? Did Merton himself know? Did Patrick Hart know if Thomas Merton knew?

I had a thousand questions and Brother Patrick was most obliging. But as we were talking about issues to which there could be no unambiguous responses, I asked the question that provoked the response I will remember the longest. I invited Brother Patrick to visit California, and our home city, to talk about Thomas Merton. It was a simple request. I had not thought of it beforehand. But it was sincere. I wanted him to accept.

The precedent upon which I was working had been formed by some apparent similarities between Merton's role in the contemporary world and Dietrich Bonhoeffer's role during World War II. It is significant that both Bonhoeffer's *Letters and Papers from Prison* and the majority of Merton's writings were conceived in cells, the former's in a prison cell, the latter's in a monastic cell. The two situations involve marked differences, but also some striking similarities, so much so that some of the literature that was produced may seem to belong to the same genre. One can assign Merton and Bonhoeffer similar functions in the process of cultural transition. Twenty-five years before Merton's death, Bonhoeffer proclaimed a "humankind come of age." Merton was on to something similar, it seemed, though the stakes could no longer be restricted to European civilization, but focused on the rapprochement between Eastern and Western cultures. Furthermore, it is intriguing that Merton, like Bonhoeffer in his *Letters and Papers from Prison*, was in touch with considerations whose greater manifestation occurred after his death. In specific ways, both had been able to sketch the configuration of a portion of the future before the future had broken through. For the religiously sensitive, both had provided a kind of sanctioned access and reliable mediation. Yet neither lived long enough to witness that which they had foretold. And neither had provided enough elaboration of their more speculative contentions to give interpretations strong assurance. Following Bonhoeffer's death, Eberhard Bethge, Bonhoeffer's friend and subsequent biographer, took it upon himself to collate the written works, explain their teaching, and identify the orientation. Bethge learned how to speak on Bonhoeffer's behalf. Bonhoeffer could be heard through Bethge.

I invited Patrick Hart to function in the same capacity. There are many people who desire to know more about Merton. They want more from him, perhaps, than he would have been able to give. They seek clarification of the intrigues he only pointed to. Insights of additional clarification are needed now that the era he had anticipated—if, indeed, he had—seems to be coming to pass.

Furthermore, some additional assistance seems important and appropriate. There is precedent for this in the Bonhoeffer/Bethge interdependence. The "Death of God" movement, the concern about "the secular city" (à la Harvey Cox's timely statement in the book by the same title), portions of Vatican II theology, as well as large segments of Jürgen Moltmann's and Wolfhart Pannenberg's theologies of hope—all very prominent developments in the sixties—seem to be consistent expressions and extensions of tendencies Bonhoeffer had suggested or set in motion. The same extensions were occurring around the personage and influence of Merton, and this phenomenon has continued particularly as the contemplative era, as it deserves now to be called, becomes more pronounced. There is need now, it seems, to put more solid information into circulation. And this includes not simply the manuscripts, but the letters, the oral history, and all of that which qualify primarily as lore. My request of Patrick Hart seemed to me to make eminent sense. It also presented itself at a propitious opportunity.

"Will you come to California?" I asked. Then, without waiting for his reply, I outlined the program possibilities and sketched several scenarios. "We could arrange a variety of meetings," I went on, "a public lecture, some informal discussions with persons on the campus and with townspeople." I wanted to convey something of the enthusiastic reception I knew he would experience were he to come.

I looked at him. Due to my anticipation and enthusiasm, I am sure I did not hear him the first time he said, "But I'm not a public speaker." I countered quickly, "But you wouldn't have to give a formal lecture or read a paper; you wouldn't even have to make a speech." I outlined the prospect. "We would invite you to sit at the table with a few carefully selected participants. They would pose some questions, and, when you felt disposed, you could respond." If the only problem we faced was his reticence to make a public speech, I was certain we could make appropriate adjustments.

I had not convinced him, however, for he continued to decline and offer reasons. "The abbot may not approve," he said softly. He added, "There is a good precedent for it." "No," I interjected, "but we can create one." "Father Louis left here one time and never returned. There must be a lesson in that for the rest of us." He managed a smile as he spoke the words, anticipating my response, I suspected. But I couldn't be sure the conclusion he had drawn was offered in total seriousness.

It was evident, though, that his resistance was firm. I retreated. I realized that I had been trying too hard. My enthusiasm had overpowered more fundamental tastes and sensitivities. Seeking to lure him into my world, in accordance with a program agenda of my own devising, I had distorted things.

He seemed to look at me with less openness now. He was no longer the person I had wanted him to be. This wasn't Eberhard Bethge's counterpart in a modern drama about religious and cultural transition. This man wasn't a participant in a scheme I had designed. It dawned on me that I really didn't know who he was. All at once, I found it curious that I wanted Patrick Hart, a man I didn't know, to tell me about Merton, whom I didn't know either. And neither knew me.

"Father Louis wouldn't like it," he added quietly. "He wouldn't want us running about the country talking about Thomas Merton. That's the last thing he'd want." My response was cautious. "But, given the fact that he's more than Father Louis now, and that Thomas Merton doesn't just belong to you, to Gethsemani, and to the Trappists, but in some profound ways has given inspiration and formation to contemporary religious understanding, indeed, even to contemporary social and cultural understanding, couldn't you bring yourself to do it?"

This was not the original request in updated form. I was seeking understanding, and I trusted he would sense that I caught what he had communicated to me. But I still found the question appropriate: "Isn't there a 'for us' in all of it? Could you do it for us?" Not the "for us" of the small symposium or conference variety, but in larger dimensions. For whom? Well, simply for those of us who had made the request. And, if not for that, for the sake of an accurate historical record. Or because of a commitment to the truth. Or for knowledge's sake. Or for history's sake. Or for a host of objective, yes, dispassionate reasons. Perhaps even for the possibility of a long-range improvement of the human condition. "Wouldn't you consider doing it for the sake of those who have no other means of access to the wisdom he symbolizes?"

His explanation was brief and firm. He said that his chief obligation and responsibility was to his monastic vocation. It was to this that he had been called. It was to this that he wanted most to remain faithful. He added that he had written a book about Thomas Merton. He was participating in various publication projects. He was not unmindful of these responsibilities. What he was doing was true to what he knew. It was also in keeping with the estimate of his friend's, Father Louis's, deepest personal counsel.

There would be no trip to California for Brother Patrick, at least not in the form in which it had been proposed, at least not for a while. There would be no symposium on Thomas Merton, no chance to test our program capabilities in this respect. And, even if there were, it could not have matched the force of the lesson that had been communicated there in the foyer of that venerable monastic setting. The request had seemed appropriate to me. But as I turned the words over in my mind, it occurred to me that its presumption—"for those of us who have no other means of access"—contained the troublesome words. It became apparent that I may have been carrying notions about how wisdom is acquired that run directly counter to the nature of the wisdom I sought.

Thomas Merton put it this way:

> The real essence of monasticism is the handing down from master to disciple of an uncommunicable experience, an experience that cannot be communicated in doctrinal terms, or in terms of philosophy, or in words. It can only be communicated on the deepest possible level. There is nothing else with the same primary importance. It is beyond the level of

psychology because there is a deeper dimension than the psychological. It is a theological dimension—if theology is seen as more than dogma, more than doctrinal formulation about something ultimate.[1]

And religious insights of the contemplative variety can hardly occur unless something of that same living environment is established or created, even for those who cannot be fulltime monks. Such insights are supported by the environment, by the schedule of daily activities, the careful ways in which time is ordered and reverenced, the reading, meditating, and cultivated sensitivity to the care of one's and other's souls, and, most important, perhaps, the work one does with one's hands.

To be sure, this realization did not come to me in a flash as I sat in the presence of Brother Patrick. It has grown over the months and years of my exposure to the monastic life. But the silence following my request for a wisdom to which I could find no other access forced me to reexamine my expectations. It became apparent that such wisdom was not Brother Patrick's to give.

My encounter with Brother Patrick left me even more perplexed about Merton's journey and bewildered about how I could ever learn what it was about. His journal tells us that he went to Asia to search for something. But his pilgrimage was much more than a religious or cultural treasure hunt, and it involved more than the desire to bring back something that might supplement and complement the riches that already belonged to monastic wisdom. To interpret the significance of his journey in any of these ways is to make his search and expectations too benign.

To place the insight in proper perspective, one must keep in mind that Merton understood the world to be undergoing a comprehensive transition. He viewed it as a changeover to a different set of arrangements, a more sophisticated mode of differentiation, and a more delicate range of energies. His many sharp criticisms of capitalism; his intrigue with Marxist diagnoses of social ills (though not necessarily with Marxist solutions); his willingness to call present economic structures obsolete, stagnant, and dead; his insistence through all of it that monastic life is integrally tied to the basis of social reform—all are signs of a growing awareness. He tended to attribute all human failings, whether individual or collective, to the deeply debilitative and disorienting effects of egocentricity. Clearly, he was flirting with the possibility of a form of "no-mindedness." But it is too simple to say that he was in the process of becoming a Buddhist. The statement is true in certain respects, but it doesn't mean that Merton was preparing himself for a radical conversion, or that he was having second thoughts regarding his devotion and commitment to the Christian faith.

At a very fundamental level, the journey to Asia can be described more accurately as a desire to perceive the nexus of life's connectedness, thus, to be obedient to the mode through which reality is engaged. Merton recognized that the West's egoistic version portrays the self as agent—that is, promoter and programmer, initiator and receptor of its own projects. And the world is the arena in which individual and collective projects are worked out. Merton perceived that this attitude badly distorts reality, eventually making one a stranger in the world, at odds with that by which one is fundamentally sustained. In wishing to identify a more resilient way of connecting, Merton also wanted to be able to penetrate beyond deception and illusion. The way was to be found in a mode of apprehension in which the distinction between subject and object was overcome.

Merton believed that this mode of engagement coalesced with mystical perception, as this had been cultivated through the centuries within the monastic and contemplative traditions, both East and West. He also recognized that his own interest belonged to the more comprehensive quest for a universal consciousness, as he called it, that was also prevalent outside monastic walls. Human consciousness was being altered profoundly, and he simply wished to witness the occurrence—to be there when it happened. It occurred as he traveled, of course; he found signs of confirmation as he went along. Indeed, the territory Merton covered over land, sea, and through the air he had already explored through the motions within his soul. Thus, whether willingly or not, deliberately or not, consciously or not, intentionally or not, Thomas Merton became both participant and catalyst in a complicated process of cultural and religious modal transformation.

To get some sense of what this meant, we must recognize, as Elena Malits has put it in her book *The Solitary Explorer: Thomas Merton's Transforming Journey*, that Merton "moved beyond the frontiers of the ordinary patterns of Cistercian life to undertake his quest for God in dialogue with those from other religious traditions." In this respect, it seems that he knew exactly what he was doing. The strategy he was pursuing was a precise one.

He was no stranger to the teachings of the various Asian religious traditions. He had written rather extensively about Zen Buddhism, in particular. He heralded the Asian monks as having penetrated "so much deeper into this than we have." He could talk at length about the attainment of the "Buddha mind," and his instincts in this regard carried him far beyond what words could say. He had studied and talked with D. T. Suzuki, among whose writings Merton was particularly fond of the book *The Zen Doctrine of No-Mind*. He approved of both the title and content of Dom Aelred Graham's book *Zen Catholicism*. All of these were subjects to which he was deeply committed.

Merton was also familiar with the theological formulae by which Christians have attempted to come to terms with religions other than their own. He was aware of the tendency to view all other religions as being either preliminary or preparatory to Christianity, and he was fully conscious of the expansionist drive within Christianity, that is, to engage in missionary activity and efforts at conversion and proselytism. He knew others had gone out to bring "the good news of Christ" to persons for whom such information is not readily available. But he appears less eager to bring something to Asia than to view his pilgrimage there, according to the pattern of the Desert Fathers, as a kind of exile within which he will find his true home.

And yet, even though Merton had firm control over such ideas and a clear sense of expectation, he proceeded in a highly original way. For he seemed almost unconcerned about conceptual formulations, being fascinated instead by the power of esthetic forms, structural arrangements, configurations, styles, and patterns. And he looked to these to enable him better to acknowledge the deepest mysteries.

Confirmation of this impression and interpretation lies in the striking observation recorded in the *Asian Journal*, after he viewed the Buddhist wood sculpture figures at Polonnaruwa in Sri Lanka. Merton writes:

> Looking at these figures, I was suddenly, almost forcibly, jerked clear out of the habitual, half-tied vision of things, and an inner clearness, clarity, as if exploding from the rocks themselves became evident and obvious.... The thing about all this is that there is no puzzle, no problem, and really no "mystery." All problems are resolved and everything is clear, simply because what matters is clear. The rock, all matter, all life ... everything is emptiness and everything is compassion.

Then follows an exclamation:

> I don't know why in my life I have ever had such a sense of beauty and spiritual validity running together in one aesthetic illumination. Surely, my Asian pilgrimage has come clear and purified itself. I mean, I know and have seen what I was obscurely looking for. I don't know what else remains but I have now seen and have pierced through the surface and

have got beyond the shadow and the disguise. . . . It says
everything; it needs nothing. And because it needs nothing
it can afford to be silent, unnoticed, undiscovered.[2]

Though the experience was rich and distinctive, it belonged to
his lifelong fascination with the power of configurational arrangements. In 1938, his master's thesis at Columbia was on
the writings of William Blake. Then, too, he was searching for a
"clarity" he described as "the glory of form shining through
matter." The same interest directed his attention to Gerard
Manley Hopkins, whose writings were to be the subject of his
proposed doctoral dissertation. He wanted to know how a poet-
mystic penetrates reality and identifies the essence of beauty.
He was taken by Hopkins's comments regarding "the unified
pattern of essential characteristics," as well as his understanding of the incarnation as being "inscaped" within the created
world.

In the same regard, it is noteworthy that Merton's two recorded experiences of personal enlightenment—the one referred
to in the *Asian Journal* and the other, cited in *The Seven Storey
Mountain*, which took place in 1933—were similar in structure.
The first time occurred while Merton was vacationing in Rome;
after visiting the museums and reading Dryden, the poems of
D. H. Lawrence, some Tauchnitz novels, and James Joyce's
Ulysses, Merton found himself becoming more intrigued by the
mosaics of the Eastern Orthodox churches. He wrote of one
mosaic in particular, one that shows "Christ coming in judgment in dark blue sky, with a suggestion of fire in the small
clouds beneath his feet":

> The effect of this discovery was tremendous. After all the
> vapid, boring, semi-pornographic statuary of the Empire,
> what a thing it was to come upon the genius of an art full of
> spiritual vitality and earnestness and power—an art that
> was tremendously serious and alive and eloquent and ur-
> gent in all that it had to say. And it was without pretentious-
> ness, without fakery; and had nothing theatrical about it.

Its solemnity was made all the more astounding by its simplicity. . . .

Merton was much taken by what he had discovered:

> I was fascinated by these Byzantine mosaics. I began to haunt the churches where they were to be found. . . . And thus without knowing anything about it I became a pilgrim. I was unconsciously and unintentionally visiting all the great shrines of Rome, and seeking out their sanctuaries with some of the eagerness and avidity and desire of a true pilgrim, though not quite for the right reason. And yet it was not for a wrong reason either. . . .

His conclusion:

> And now for the first time in my life I began to find out something of Who this Person was that men called Christ. It was obscure, but it was a true knowledge of Him, in some sense, truer than I knew and truer than I would admit. It was in Rome that my conception of Christ was formed. It was there I first saw Him. . . . [3]

These two instances of enlightenment must be interpreted with reference to each other. Both the insights and the commentaries on them are remarkably similar. In both, there is a combined occurence: esthetic illumination bathed in religious significance. And each provides access to a world to which entry can be found only after one has undertaken passage or pilgrimage from more familiar surroundings. The first was entry into Christianity, significantly through the visual pathway of Eastern Orthodoxy. The second, in Sri Lanka, involved Buddhist influences. Each time he reached out for a truth not altogether his own. But the second time it became impossible for him to carry the truth "back home," for "home" was transformed into a much more inclusive orbit than the Western world.

Yet, at Polonnaruwa, the religious insight and the esthetic illumination were fused, becoming virtually interchangeable.

Using Hopkins's language, it is entirely plausible that Merton perceived the deepest mystery to be "inscaped" in the wood sculptures. Surely he recognized its power because it exhibited esthetic consonance with a distinctive cultural way of life.

The Benedictine monk and scholar, Jean Leclercq, who is an expert on the life and times of twelfth- and thirteenth-century France, was in Bangkok at the same time, in 1968, and a participant in the same conference. Indeed, it was through Leclercq's invitation that Merton went there.

Leclercq returned to Sri Lanka in the early autumn of 1980 and went to Polonnaruwa to view the very same Buddhist wood sculptures Merton described in his journal. Being a close friend of Merton's, Leclercq had the latter's description of the event in mind as he returned to the site. I understand that he read the passages aloud to himself as he stood in the same place Merton did some twelve years before.

I saw Father Leclercq shortly after he returned, and, as I had done previously with Brother Patrick, I asked if he could convey something more of Merton's insight.

"What do you think he saw?" I asked Leclercq. "Was he looking for some form or conception of Christ in the Buddhist wood sculptures?" I put the question this way because this was the sequence of the first disclosure in Rome from the Byzantine mosaics. I wondered if the second experience followed the same pattern.

"No, I do not think so," Father Leclercq replied quickly and confidently.

I followed with another question. "Was there any specific Christian content or insight in it for Merton?"

Again Leclercq answered in the negative. But we were both dissatisfied with the way I had phrased the question. Its parochial nature violated Merton's intention to discover a more expansive and human, but no less specific, perspective to foster the religious quest.

"Well, then, what did he see?" I asked with some impatience.

The gentle monk responded with a twinkle in his eye. "I think he saw what was there."

"Not Christ in Buddhist form, not the Buddha through Christian eyes, but simply what was there?" I repeated.

"Yes," Father Leclercq nodded, smiling broadly now, "but it was Christ who taught him how to see. And he learned how to see it as it is."

The conversation ended. I might have been disappointed with its outcome, for the response was elusive. Yet I recognized that my question had been answered as profoundly as it could be. To perceive reality as it truly is is the deepest aspiration of the contemplative vision. It is the primary catalyst of the monastic impulse. But no one can provide much more elaborate communication until a person, according to monastic principles, perceives it with his or her own eyes.

What can be said beyond this in more general terms is that Thomas Merton sensed the arrival of a new and dramatically revised set of religious conditions. He went to Asia to greet its coming. And in the years following his death, what had been only dimly prefigured has moved much closer to the center of consciousness for Easterners and Westerners alike.

Merton didn't live to witness the culmination. Dietrich Bonhoeffer didn't live to see his day either. And the same is true of Martin Luther King, Jr., whose exclamation—"I know and have seen what I was obscurely looking for, for I have pierced through the shadow and the disguise, and I have now seen"—carries the tone of Merton's notes recorded in *Asian Journal*. Each was in touch with insights that were held under something less than firm control. For Merton, the means of access was through the imaginative and conceptual possibilities implicit in significant patterns of structural arrangement. It took some time to translate the esthetic insight into appropriate words. But this is exactly what one should expect of disclosures of this quality and intensity, especially those that emanate, as Merton attested, from places where visible and invisible intersect.

4

TAIZÉ

Taizé is a place. It is also an idea. And it is a spirit, a tendency, a movement. Taizé is a distinctive spirit emanating from a gentle place guided by a venerable idea.

Fifty thousand young people come to Taizé for Easter Sunday services each year. Between five and ten thousand are present each day throughout the summer. They come either singly or in groups, from everywhere. Some come with nothing but a few belongings, sleeping bags, tents; some come without money. They come on foot, on bicycles, by bus. They stay for a brief time, a few days, a week, sometimes longer.

Taizé is an ashram of distinctively (though not narrowly) Christian orientation. It is a new place that has captured the enthusiasm of literally tens of thousands of young people, not only in Europe, but throughout the world. It is impressive in the attention it attracts and retains, a phenomenon of the sixties and seventies, very much the product of extended and refined counterculture aspirations, directed most specifically to religious, social, and cultural renewal. These are the dramatic visible features of the place. But the fuller story may be even more interesting and important.

The Taizé community was not the first monastic community to become established in the area. About seven kilometers away in a valley lie the ruins of the Abbey of Cluny. This famous Benedictine abbey was established in 910. Its church, built between 1090 and 1130, was the largest in the world until Saint Peter's Bascilica in Rome was built. From this monastic, religious, and administrative center sprang a large network of monasteries, all following the customs, reforms, disciplines, and liturgical practices of the mother house. In time, more than a thousand Cluniac houses had spread over western Europe, all strictly bound to the abbot and chapter of Cluny. Hence, Cluny was the catalyst of significant church reform in the eleventh century. Eventually, the town was taken by the troops of Louis XI in 1471, and the abbey again suffered during the religious wars of the sixteenth century. As an abbey it was closed in 1790, but portions of the original enclosure remain. Today's visitors can perceive the splendor that once was.

More ancient than Cluny, and, in certain respects, more venerable, are the Romanesque churches in the area, one or two of which are immediately adjacent to the new monastic enclosure. When one surveys all of this—allowing historical memory to dance quickly from the phenomenon of Cluny to the still powerful and eloquent achievements of the earlier settlement, and the vibrant new twentieth-century monastic community—the impression is like that from three visual slides, viewed one after the other. Each one symbolizes the cultural and religious aspirations of the time. Each one is impressive in its distinctiveness. Yet all belong to the same visual set. It is almost as if the present community is a deliberate expression of the interpenetration of complex processes of cultural permanence and change. For the new monastery, built upon the rubble and the recollection of a very old place, exists in temporary quarters, in the main. Except for the buildings from former eras that it inhabits, and the rather inexpensive and temporary-looking buildings that have been erected recently, Taizé has only a complement of tents. Large tents. Small tents. Colorful tents. Army-khaki tents. Picnic tables. Expedient shower stalls. Rudimentary dishwashing facilities. A bookstore. A post office. Little children playing on the gravel roads. Domesticated dogs. Flowers. Light blue sky above extending far enough south to begin reflecting the yellow and orange hues of the Mediterranean world. Tall grasses in the surrounding fields.

The scene gives the appearance of an oversized and not closely regimented military occupation after hostilities have ceased, or a scout camp for college- and postcollege-age men and women. It is a transient community, a way station for a monastic people in pilgrimage. The symbolism is apt, for Taizé tries deliberately and self-consciously to pursue the goals of effective social action from within the resources of a deeply nourished contemplative tradition. It is primarily Protestant and Catholic in its terminology and literature; yet it is open to the insights and practices of other religious traditions, particularly those that have grown up in Eastern or Asian cultures. It is deliberately nonparochial. However, as a new and flexible monastic community, Taizé also derives its life from the legacy of layer upon layer of Western civilization. Thus, it is ecumenical in its Christianity, cross-cultural and implicitly trans-religious in temperament and scope, summoning the Western world both backward and forward to priorities that have been misplaced or need to be discovered.

The key to the specific meaning of Taizé lies in the work and vision of Roger Schutz, founder of the community and present prior, spiritual counselor, and veritable pastor and priest for hosts of persons throughout the world. Indeed, the story of Taizé and the biography of Roger Schutz coalesce in perfect symmetry—a remarkable example of the intersection of an individual life-cycle with a particular moment or segment of history.

Born on May 12, 1915, near Neuchâtel in Switzerland, Schutz was attracted early to the study of theology, pursuing this course of studies at Lausanne and Strasbourg. Prior to the outbreak of the Second World War, in 1939, he was elected president of the Protestant Student Federation in Lausanne. He utilized his office to found a prayer and study group, a kind of "third order" called the "the Grande Communauté." The group met monthly for prayer and discussion. Thus, it was in search of a house for the group that Schutz journeyed to Burgundy, exploring possibilities there as well as in Switzerland, near Geneva. He settled upon Taizé for reasons Rex Brico summarizes in his perceptive account, *Taizé. Brother Roger and his Community.*

> So in August 1940, Roger travelled to Burgundy, where some of his mother's relatives were still living. After several days of searching for a house he found two excellent possibilities: one over the Swiss border near Geneva and another in the neighborhood of Bourg. The first one included, in addition to a farm, a tiny chapel where Francis de Sales had once celebrated the Eucharist. The other stood at the foot of a hill and looked out over rich farmland. With his sense of spiritual beauty, Roger was enchanted by the possibilities. But he continued his journey, since he knew that was not why he had come to France. When he arrived in the town of Cluny, a lawyer drew his attention to the nearby village of Taizé, where a house large enough for his purposes had lain unoccupied for a long time. He rode out to it on his bicycle and found a tiny hamlet, half in ruins, almost completely abandoned by its inhabitants. In addition to the war, a series of bad harvests had turned the land into a desert. It was a hopeless miserable sight. An old peasant woman, who kept the keys, showed him the house. When Roger asked where he could get something to eat, she said, 'Here, with me'. During the meal she whispered, 'Buy the house and stay here! We're all alone!' And that tipped the scales. Roger now says: 'I chose Taizé because the woman was poor. Christ speaks through the poor and it's good to listen to them. Anyone who begins with the poorest of the poor is not likely to go wrong . . . .

Brico summarizes the outcome:

> The rest of the group accepted Roger's decision to settle in Taizé, though they would have preferred a place in Switzerland. In September he bought the house through a

lawyer in Cluny. Interestingly enough, on the very day he
signed the deed, the impoverished owner of the house,
Madame de Brie, was in Lyons ending a novena she was offering for its sale. A totally unexpected telegram brought
her misery to an end.

The connection with the Abbey of Cluny was made explicit
from the start. The group decided to call the new settlement the
House of Cluny. Brico's account continues:

> In December 1940, after the necessary preparations, the
> Grande Communauté was able to hold its first meeting in
> their new quarters, which was called the House of Cluny.[1]

It is evident that Schutz felt close identification with the area
from the first. Writing in his diary, he describes one early morning in Taizé this way:

> 28 July
>
> Four in the morning. Went out for a moment as I do almost
> every day at dawn. The star-studded sky is growing pale. A
> dim dawn begins to break. A month before at this hour the
> northern sky was transparent, clear green, then rapidly
> ablaze. Now autumn mists are already toning down much of
> the light's brilliance. In a few hours I shall again be taking
> the path along the hill as far as the church—the path I was
> walking along yesterday evening, pausing to breathe in the
> night—a burning eastern night. Today everything is gentle
> again. The distant views are light and peaceful. I am truly
> restored to the Burgundy that bore my mother's ancestors.[2]

On the other hand, it was the possibility of being in a place
where he might assist refugees of the war that most attracted
Schutz to Taizé. Years later, Schutz made this entry in his journal recalling the initial period in Taizé:

> 4 September
>
> Relived intensely an evening in the summer of 1942, when I
> was still on my own in Taizé. I was sitting writing at a small

table. I knew I was in danger because of the political refugees I was sheltering in the house. The risk that I would be
arrested was considerable. Members of the civilian police
force had repeatedly made raids and questioned me. That
evening, with fear in the pit of my stomach, a prayer took
hold of me. I said it to God without really understanding
what I was saying, "Take my life if you think fit, but let
what has begun here continue." Yet what had been begun in
those two years? Principally a welcoming house and prayer
in solitude.[3]

As it turned out, Schutz was forced to flee from Taizé in 1942.
He returned to Switzerland, rented a house near the cathedral
in Geneva, and joined with three other men—Max Thurian,
Pierre Souverain, and Daniel de Montmollin—to live a life of
celibacy and the sharing of community goods. The most direct
influence was that of Saint Francis of Assisi. Later Schutz said
of him:

There is one example in history of an authentic reform: Saint
Francis of Assisi. He suffered for the Church, loving it as
Christ loves it. It would have been easy for him to pass
harsh judgments on the institutions, the customs, and the
callous attitudes of some of his fellow Christians. But that is
precisely what he refused to do. He chose instead to die to
himself, waiting with burning patience until at last his love-
filled waiting brought about renewal.[4]

Devoted to the example of Saint Francis, the four men pledged
to pray together each day in one of the chapels of the cathedral.
During this period of time, Roger Schutz was working on his
thesis, "The Monastic Ideal before Saint Benedict and Its Con-
formity to the Gospel," an ideal he believed lay open to Protestants too.

He was ordained in 1943, returned to Taizé in 1944. By then,
the German occupation had ended. But the need to deal with
refugees from the war was just as great. Schutz utilized the
community's facilities primarily to take in children who had
lost their parents in the war.

The next years found the brothers working the land and continuing to provide hospitality to refugees, strangers, and pilgrims.

Easter Day, 1949, was a significant milestone in the life of the community. On that day, seven men pledged themselves permanently to live in community. They took the traditional monastic vows, committing themselves to the rules of celibacy, community of goods, and the acceptance of authority. On that day too, Roger became prior of the community, taking the name by which he has been known since, Brother Roger, prior of Taizé. The ceremony took place in the small Romanesque church adjacent to the monastic compound. Permission to utilize the village church had been granted earlier by the papal nuncio in Paris, Angelo Roncalli, later Pope John XXIII, who was a great friend and supporter of the Taizé community.

Growth and expansion were steady. The monks became adept at what they were doing. Their work and devotional life attracted considerable interest. Many more persons came to live with the community. Some of them took the vows.

In 1952–53, Brother Roger prepared a Rule of Taizé, the spirit of which is captured in the following line from its Preamble:

> This Rule contains only the minimum necessary for a community seeking to build itself in Christ, and to give itself up to a common service of God. This resolve to lay down only the essential disciplines involves a risk: that your liberty may become a pretext for living according to your own impulses.

Clearly, Brother Roger wanted to strike a balance between personal freedom and community obligation.

> You fear that a common rule may stifle your personality, whereas its purpose is to free you from useless shackles, so that you may better bear the responsiblities of the ministry and make better use of its boldness. Like every Christian,

you must accept the tension between the total freedom given by the Holy Spirit and the impossibilities in which you find yourself due to your neighbour's and your own fallen nature.

You would narrow your understanding of the Gospel, if, for fear of losing your life, you were to spare yourself. Unless a grain of wheat dies, you cannot hope to see your own self open out in the fullness of Christian life.

Then, seeking to bolster their aspirations, Brother Roger admonishes:

Never stand still; go forward with your brothers, run towards the goal in the footsteps of Christ. His path is a way of light: I am, but also you are the light of the world.... For the pure brightness of Christ to enter into you, it is not enough to gaze on it as though you were a disembodied spirit; you must commit yourself resolutely, in body and soul, on this path.

These are some of the ways they were to show the same:

Be a sign of joy and of brotherly love among men.

Open yourself to all that is human and you shall see any vain desire to flee from the world vanish from your heart. Be present to the time in which you live; adapt yourself to the conditions of the moment. O Father, I pray you, not to take them out of the world, but keep them from evil.

Love the dispossessed, all those who, living amid man's injustice, thirst after justice. Jesus had a special concern for them. Have not fear of being disturbed by them.

Show your parents deep affection and help them to recognize, through its very quality, the absolute imperative of your vocation.

Love your neighbour, whatever may be his political or religious beliefs.

Always, the goal was to assist healing the divisions within Christendom:

> Never resign yourself to the scandal of the separation of
> Christians, all who so readily confess love for their neigh-
> bour, and yet remain divided. Be consumed with burning
> zeal for the unity of the Body of Christ.[5]

Through the years, monastic life became more regularized.
The brothers were sent out, two by two, according to the New
Testament command, to live and work in surrounding communities. In places where they resided, they established "fraternities." Today, these fraternities exist throughout the
world.

In 1977, the community added an "itinerant fraternity," con-
sisting of groups of persons, two or four in number, who travel
from place to place, understanding themselves to be living out
the compulsions of the gospel in its original and radical simplicity. As these monastic developments were occurring beyond
the Taizé region, visitors and pilgrims continued to find their
way to the small village. Reflecting on the large influx, Brother
Roger wrote in his diary:

> February, 1969
>
> When I chose the village of Taizé in 1940, I was alone . . . .
> For a long period our life was marked not by isolation but by
> an accepted solitude. Nonetheless, from the very start our
> life at Taizé has been interwoven by encounters with others.
> After twenty years of common life we were thrown, so to
> speak, into the public arena. It has taken seven years, from
> 1962 to 1969, to circumscribe what was happening to us.
>
> But while welcoming large numbers, we have always found
> ways to establishing zones of peace on the hill. I suspect
> that such simple values—silence, and also the love for things,
> for domestic animals—strengthen a creative capacity in us.[6]

In the same year, the community, which already had vowed
brothers from Reformed, Lutheran, and Anglican traditions,
took in its first Roman Catholic member. Others, including
priests, soon followed, with Cardinal Marty, archbishop of Par-

is, giving his approval. In the main, Catholics and Protestants
live in harmony. But when it comes to celebrating the Eucharist, walls of division or distinction still pertain. The Catholic
Mass and the Protestant Eucharistic service are celebrated at
the same time in different chapels in the crypt of the church.
The elements are distributed in various places near the altar.
Catholics receive near the icon of the Virgin Mary, Protestants
near the icon of the Cross. Reflecting Brother Roger's feelings
about this arrangement, Brico writes: "Brother Roger, though
an ordained pastor, does not celebrate the Eucharist any
longer, thus questioning by a personal gesture this state of af-
fairs."[7]

Easter Day, 1970, brought a significant development. On
that Sunday, Brother Roger announced to the twenty-five hun-
dred persons gathered on the hill that "we are going to hold a
council of youth." Brico describes the reason and the occasion:

So Easter 1970 was the starting-point for the long desert
march which the Council was to become. Young people who
had met one another at a deeper level at Taizé remained in
touch when they returned home. Each one started out from
his or her own situation, from a Church group, a Third World
action group, or even a trade union. People came together
regularly, visited one another, or met in Taizé. Others left
for distant lands, in order to strengthen existing contacts
and to form new ones. Young people from Brazil, France,
and Cameroon travelled through Belgium and Luxembourg;
a boy from Sri Lanka and two from France visited Australia;
an Indian travelled through the United States. There was
even more correspondence by letter. To handle this flood of
letters, the community had to open its own post office. Slowly a common awareness of a new life-style began to grow, for
which Taizé served as a sounding-board, the antenna to
gather news of what was springing up here and there. From
time to time a new intercontinental team of young people in
Taizé went through the letters and other reports. In that
way in the days before Easter 1971 a new message took
shape. It attempted to answer the question: what are the
consequences of a festival announced a year ago? The team
answered: 'It implies a struggle to let all take part in that

same liberating festival.... Becoming aware of oppressions. Committing our energies to breaking with situations where man is victim of man. Rejecting privileges. Refusing the hunt for success. Furthering communion among all. Finding liberation—our own and our neighbour's both near and far away. Being released ourselves so as to secure others' release.' How? So that the news may pass from one to another, so that little by little it may bring back to life all that is inert among Christians. We are still situated in the hidden, underground movement of the Church. We are being led to live incognito, like leaven hidden in the dough, like seed buried in the ground, seeking poverty of heart, always using poor means, without gold or silver.[8]

On Easter Day, 1972, sixteen thousand visitors from more than eighty countries were present in Taizé. Grass-roots communities began to spring up. Eighteen thousand people came to Taizé for the Easter celebration in 1973. And on August 30, 1974, forty thousand people came to Taizé for the official opening of the Council of Youth. Writing about the day in his journal, Brother Roger describes his expectations:

30 August 1974

The day has come, this opening day of the Council of Youth, the day when we all long to say: open yourself to understand each person fully, every woman and man, made of the same stuff as you and who like you, searches, struggles, creates, prays.

The day has come after long waiting, in common searching, with all the tensions which that involves. And what has finally prevailed has been trusting love.

On August 20, 1940, when I arrived in this human wasteland, there was nothing to suggest these days when forty thousand young people would be gathered together at Taizé. And all those far away, as well, those very dear to us who are reduced to silence, imprisoned, suffering because of the Gospel and their struggle for justice and freedom.

With all of them, with people from every part of the world, we are being called to a life that exceeds all our hopes.[9]

From that day, the spirit of Taizé has become increasingly internationalized. There have been celebration meetings of the Council of Youth on every continent. Brother Roger himself has traveled extensively. He has formed common bond and common cause with Mother Teresa, whom he has visited, and who has visited and stayed in Taizé. The Taizé brothers have traveled far and wide too. Characteristically, when they visit a community, they live with the poor; they identify with the oppressed. Brother Roger has spent time among the poorest of the poor in Calcutta, and in Hong Kong. He has spent time in prayer in Bari, in southern Italy, among poor fishermen and masons. He is deeply involved in the problems of the Third World.

Wherever it has come to life, the spirit of Taizé has expressed itself as a concern for the refugees of injustice and the victims of the world's disharmonies. Brother Roger originally thought of this problem in distinctively European terms, having been deeply affected by the ravages of the two world wars. In the years since the founding of Taizé, the same sensitivity has focused particularly on the victims of injustice within the world's poorer nations.

The pictures on the walls of the monastery illustrate this incentive. One gathers from several commemorative photographs that Brother Roger seems very pleased that the community has received the blessing of Pope Paul VI. But the pictures that show him to be even more jubilant are ones in which he is walking side by side with Mother Teresa.

The monks of Taizé believe that the imperatives of the New Testament should be lived out in radical terms. As such, the community wishes to affirm that the world is being reinvented, the chief symbolism for which is the Easter story. Accordingly, throughout its history, the formative and commemorative events have occurred (or have been announced) on Easter Sunday. This is a long-standing tradition in the Cluny valley as well. In a perceptive essay on the mood and temper of Cluniac monastic religion, E. Delaruelle refers to Cluny's "resurrection-centered spirituality." Contrasting the spirituality of the Crusades (wherein the ideal was to suffer and die in the very place where Christ had suffered and died) with the attitude prevailing at Cluny, Delaruelle writes:

> The best representative of the Cluniac mentality is St. Odilo, in his sermons. It is not merely that he shows no sign of any special interest in the Holy Land; more significant is the fact that he consistently presents the Christian mysteries in their glorious aspect. In his work the epiphany is not a picturesque scene from Christ's infancy at the moment of the redemptive incarnation, as it is for the Gothic artists; rather, it is a majestic scene, indeed a theophany, to be associated with our Lord's baptism and the miracle at Cana. The resurrection is approached less as an event than as a mystery of new creation in the Spirit, and the same is true of the ascension and pentecost. Above all does this spirituality show itself when Odilo is speaking of the passion: the cross is for him no shameful instrument of torture, but a symbol of triumph. . . .
>
> Jotsald tells us that for Odilo Cluny was the promised land, and catches the spirit of Cluny as he says it: what need is there to go seeking Christ in the Holy Land? We are in Jerusalem already, a Jerusalem lit up with glory.[10]

It is apparent that the Taizé community sustains the same resurrection-centered spirituality.

Today there are some eighty-five monks in residence in the Taizé community, with other members scattered throughout the world, working in places of human need, and keeping in touch with one another through the newsletter that is published monthly by the community. Taizé's theme is *ora et labora*, prayer and work. It is also its reason for being, trying as it can to respond to human suffering and need, identifying with the underprivileged and downtrodden in the spirit of Mother Teresa.

The thousands of young people who come each year are drawn

by the presence of the permanent monastic community. They participate in the three liturgies that are scheduled throughout the day—in the morning, at noon, and in the evening. And as they do this, it is suggested that they be conscious of the prayers that are offered by their counterparts throughout the world, who have pledged to pause for prayer, wherever they may be, three times each day—in the morning, at noon, and in the evening.

The liturgies are simple, innovative, many of them borrowed from other places (oftentimes from progressive Catholic monasteries), others created on location, sometimes spontaneously. Rules of silence are strictly enforced, during, before, and immediately after worship. Encouragement in this direction is tendered by signs placed strategically near the doors of the sanctuary: "SILENCE." "SILENCIO." "RUHE."

Before and after liturgy, the people gathered care for their own needs, carry on quiet conversation, engage in discussions of relevant sociopolitical topics, strum guitars in front of the tents, and enjoy one another's company. Even though there are many people, it is a quiet place, a subdued scene, as befits an ashram, or a monastery, or the ruins of a Roman settlement, on the hill overlooking the valley of Cluny.

I asked some of the Taizé pilgrims why they had come. What were they looking for? What did they expect to find? Why were they attracted to Taizé? I received identical answers from several of them. They came to be strengthened by the others, to be together in a place where they can know, feel, see, and realize the support of the others who view life the way they do. "We feel like a minority in the world" one of them offers. And some others nod in agreement. "We come here to be together, and to talk together, to be with the monks, so that we might be strengthened to go back."

"Do you really mean 'minority'?" I ask. "'Minority' in the sense in which the word is most commonly used?"

The answer is immediate and emphatic, "Yes, of course."

And the others indicate their agreement. I am thinking of racial minorities, ethnic minorities, economic minorities, religious minorities. But they seem to be referring to an underrepresented group, persons who feel alienated from prevailing currents in the dominant sociocultural world.

"Will you tell me, if you can, why you feel this way?" I ask. There is a long pause, some concerned looks, and glances back and forth. Then one of them responds, "Sir, this is something we cannot explain. This is something we need not explain. It is our basic premise."

It is curious and magnificently paradoxical. Feeling like minority persons in the world, they aspire to be persons of a new age—an age to be ordered according to an altered, challenging set of human priorities. Further, they understand that the larger world—in which they will take their places as members of the minority—must be redesigned to acknowledge these compelling facts. Some profess this in radical terms, contending that former worlds will never again be realistic human possibilities for them. Others approve of the language Theodore Roszak used when referring to "the sifting down" of the top heavy and toxic institutions of an exhausted empire" into "civilized, durable communities where a vital, new sense of human identity and destiny can take root." They know all about the dawning of the Age of Aquarius. But it is no longer enough to challenge the status quo, shock humankind, or simply and naively to question authority. The world needs assistance in moving to a new place.

Taizé is a testing ground, a place within which strategies are planned, and objectives conceived not only concerning ways in which the massive problems might be approached, but also regarding ways through which the human spirit can remain alive in a world grown exceedingly complex. It is also evidence that the durable objectives of the counterculture did not die. They may have been pushed to the periphery of society. They may have gone underground, become less obvious, more subtle, and, perhaps, more sophisticated.

It was said of the original House of Cluny that it "formed a little world, a microcosm of the greater world." Whether the same can be said of Taizé only time and hope can tell. But, for the time being, the men and women of the new House of Cluny, as Thomas Merton counseled, are "holding together what they are not yet able to put together." In doing so, they give evidence that the monastic impulse remains in vital contact with life's moving forces.

5

SPENCER

"**N**o more difficult than being an effective natural father," he responded. He rubbed his large hands together. His eyes twinkled. He was a big man by all standards, nearly six-and-a-half-feet tall. Very strong looking. Full bearded. Inquisitive. Substantial. Eager to know that his enthusiasms are shared. A New Yorker. A descendant of several generations of American Catholics. A claimant to a portion of the legacy of the Quaker tradition from his father's side. Had I only seen him, not knowing who he was, I would have believed it had someone told me he was a spiritual teacher. His demeanor showed it. And he was responding to a question I had raised about the trials and perplexities of being a "spiritual father." I had found his ascription intriguing, and asked him how all of this sat with him.

We had come to this point in the discussion in a roundabout way. I had come to Saint Joseph's Abbey, near Spencer, Massachusetts, simply out of interest in seeing what is reported to be one of the Trappists' most vital and impressive monastic centers. The abbey itself is set atop a hill off from the left side of the road, three or four miles north of downtown Spencer. The road from Spencer weaves through a series of gently rolling hills in a lightly populated area. It was snowing at the time of my visit. As I drove along, the headlights of the car illumined the whiteness that was all around. There were icy patches on the two-lane road, and smoke curled from chimneys in the nineteenth-century French-style houses along the roadside. "CHRIST-MAS TREES FOR SALE" signs arose along the nightscape, in front of configurations of wintered trees on the hills. The abbey's stately porter's lodge by the entrance to the site, in well-kept white enamel, was a good preview of the tastefulness that followed. It was December 17, an anniversary of the burial of Thomas Merton.

I knocked on the door of the guesthouse. Within seconds, I was greeted with much exuberance, and in three swift minutes I was placed in the care of Father Basil Pennington, my host. Immediately calling me by my first name, he explained that we would have conversation after the vesper service. The reading of that office was just minutes away. He invited me to sit adjacent to the monks in the choir. I followed him as he walked briskly through the hallways, down a series of serpentine inner trails in broken darkness. Without a guide I wouldn't have been able to find my way. All was dark and silent, with only a modest quantity of heat.

Following vespers, we walked back down through the dark corridors to Father Basil's office. To begin with, he offered me some fine Portuguese wine and mixed nuts. He had just returned from an eight-month residency in a monastery on Mount Athos. On his return to the States, he had had an audience in Rome with the Pope. Crackling with ideas, questions, and suggestions, he fascinated me from the first, and I understood why others had been attracted to him. He is cross-culturally conversant too; he wanted to talk about correspondences between Catholic, Orthodox, as well as Asian forms of spirituality and monastic life. Being well read, he gave me advice about what to look for in the writings of some of the medieval mystics, particularly those who belong to the Cistercian tradition. As director of studies in his house, he had a tutor's opinion about which of the mystical writers should be encountered first, which later, and which only under the guidance of someone proficient. Displaying a gift for accuracy of detail, he was a gold mine of information. He had known Thomas Merton well, had collaborated with him in the founding of the series of books and studies named Cistercian Studies (now available through Western Michigan University). He showed me a postcard he had received "from Tom," written from Bangkok the day before Merton was killed. This thought prompted him to sweep through the sequence of events and ideas recorded in the *Asian Journal*. I wanted him to say and write more about Merton, but I sensed that he was too close to be able to discern what others would wish him to say. In addition, he had come to know the Maharishi Mahesh Yogi. He had interviewed many of the roshis of the Tibetan Buddhist tradition. He had recently given a lecture at Yale Divinity School at the invitation of Henri Nouwen, who is on the faculty. An organizer of conferences, some of them interreligious, he made one feel he was very well connected.

Father Basil wanted most to talk about the "prayer of centering," a subject on which he had published two books, *Daily We Touch Him* (1977) and *Centering Prayer* (1980).[1] I had known of the book and the practice, having heard about both from Alan McCoy, a Franciscan, at the Old Mission in Santa Barbara. Father Basil emphasized two characteristics of the practice. First, it provides linkage with the Christian religion for those persons who, after having been exposed to Asian religious currents, return to the West in search of religious and spiritual equivalents. Second, it has a fundamental place in the training of novices within the Trappist order, and in the spiritual renewal programs offered to priests and nuns within the Catholic Church. I sensed that Father Basil was much taken by the technique. He explained how it offered an alternative, or perhaps a complement, to the procedures of transcendental meditation, an orientation he believed offered very great benefits. He had been through all of it, he said. He had been initiated into the ways of transcendental meditation. He was acquainted with selected aspects of both Hindu and Buddhist forms of spirituality. And he would have been prepared to pursue a long, involved, intricate, comparative analysis of religious traditions East and West, focusing particularly on their respective meditational and spiritual practices. I was ready to indulge him in this, but I was less interested in hearing him explain his theology than in hearing more of his impressions about the dominant religious and cultural tendencies of the present age.

For, like so many others, he had become fascinated with the generation of young Americans born shortly after the close of World War II. He had been following the development and expression of their interests through the turbulent sixties and into the calmer seventies. And he was trying to make sense of the dramatic changes they had been exhibiting. He was particularly concerned to understand why many of them had turned to Eastern forms of religious and personal awareness. And he was testing several possible explanations.

He offered a simple hypothesis. He suggested that the Eastern spiritual teachers commended themselves because there is evident harmony between the truths they teach and the love they transmit and share. He didn't intend this judgment to be exhaustive. He wasn't being patronizing either. But he contrasted this situation with one that is more familiar in the West.

He added that he believed many persons had missed receiving this combination of resources from their parents or guardians during the early formative periods in their lives. And he ventured that frequently the spiritual master is the first person of real or vested authority to offer appropriate amends.

It is an intriguing idea: love transmitted by the spiritual teacher fills a vacuum created by the absence or confusion of parental love, or, perhaps, by ambivalent authority. An absence or deficiency at an early stage of life is compensated for later on, if it can be, and in a different form. This implies that the reawakening of the contemplative tradition came about when it did, at least in part, because a particular generation of young persons—both advantaged and disadvantaged—had come to a stage in their lives when they became proficient in making their deepest needs known. In Father Basil's perceptions lies a reenactment of the entire Freudian drama regarding the workings of displacement, sublimation, transference, projection, and complicated, intricate substitutionary roles.

Wishing him to carry the thought further, I asked whether his own vocation had been influenced by this interpretation of the interdependence of religious, psychological, and sociological factors. "Do you understand yourself to be a spiritual father?" I ventured. He paused, looked at me quizzically, wondering, I suspected, whether something more was lurking in the question. The answer came slowly. The words were measured. Yes, he had been asked to act as one repeatedly. But his vocation in this area had come as a great surprise, like a gift unexpectedly bestowed, to the utter astonishment of the recipient.

Suspecting that it must involve large demands on him personally, and that he wanted to say so, I asked, "What is it like to be a spiritual father?"

This time the response was swift. "It is no more difficult, I would suppose, than being an effective natural father!"

Then Father Basil turned things about and began questioning me. He asked me about my own role as a father—albeit a natural (or biological) father—a different form of fatherhood than the one about which we had been speaking, but a subject that belonged to the discussion. He observed that this more common form of paternity carries great responsibility too. And before I could say very much, he leaned forward, speaking quietly, as if sharing a secret, "We are all of us sons, sons in search of the Father."

I was treated next to Father Basil's interpretation of some of the mystical passages in the Fourth Gospel, passages referring to the process of "going to the Father." But the conversation soon became very much less intense as he turned to lessons that can be drawn from the history of monastic and mystical religion in the West. He was trying to place contemporary developments in the larger picture, and he wished to invoke the perspective of several centuries of Christian history in the West, as envisioned through attitudes nurtured by Cistercian experience. The time had come, he proposed, to tell the story of the development of the Christian religion in the West in a new way. Too little is known or acknowledged about the importance of the roles of spiritual father and spiritual mother, particularly from the time of the twelfth century on. He believed that too many historians—concentrating on institutions or major intellectual motifs—overlook factors like these. He offered that only when the scholar keeps such important psychosocial dynamics in mind can he begin to get "the feel" of a century.

Amplification of these observations and judgments came the following morning over breakfast with the respected abbot of Saint Joseph's Abbey, Father Thomas Keating. I began by rehearsing some of the impressions I had gotten from the conversation of the night before, particularly those that utilized historical and cultural analyses as a means of coming to terms with the new interest in mystical religion and the monastic way of life in his last quarter of the twentieth century. I gathered from Father Thomas's responses that he and Father Basil had been working closely in developing the impressions and interpretations they were lending me.

Abbot Thomas said that there was a time earlier in the history of the Western world when there was a fitting correspondence between the dictates of the human heart and the power of the human mind. That correspondence was prevalent during the time of Cistercian beginnings in the twelfth century. It was made explicit in the writings of Saint Bernard of Clairvaux. One finds it, too, in Cistercian literature, probably even in Cistercian architecture and artistic expressions. The entire tradition is witness to the principle of this aspiration.

Subsequently, the abbot continued, and as all analyses of this sort proceed, "something happened." I prepared myself to hear a series of critical remarks about the devastation wrought by the Reformation, the rise of Protestantism, and the ensuing fragmentation of Christendom's spiritual, theological, and ecclesiastical unity. But the criticism didn't come. Yes, Father Thomas referred to "the great schism"—his description of the Reformation. But it was not the events associated with the rise of Protestantism that lay at fault as much as developments within the more specifically Roman Catholic fold of the Christian religion. In Father Thomas's view, it was during the Counter-Reformation that the dominant form of spiritual formation, originally designed to come to terms with all components of the human personality—heart, mind, soul, will, and the habits of each together—became weakened, truncated, one-sided, imbalanced, and thus impoverished. Partly under the influence of the Jesuits, he believed, and for very persuasive reasons, the *vita comtemplativa* came to be construed more and more exclusively in intellectual—as opposed to affective—terms. All of this served as prelude to the great discussions of the Enlightenment period regarding the relation of reason and the passions of the human heart. Signs of this conflict are explicit in Pascal's statment, "The heart has reasons that reason doesn't know." In seventeenth-century France, the same difficulties fed the controversies surrounding Quietism, the validity of Molinos's orientation, the place of Jean-Pierre de Caussade, and the emphases of Francis de Sales. The implication is that the issues that surfaced at that time have never been completely resolved. It is significant, too, that the classic mystical treatises, for the most part, were produced prior to the close of the seventeenth century. Significant works were written subsequently, but the time of the great contemplative flowering in the Western world had come to an end in the eighteenth century. Eventually, except where the tradition was kept alive, the subject was pushed from prominence. The legacy remains, of course, but in obscure fashion.

Considering the present era in light of this analysis, Father Thomas believes that persons today are being motivated to reach back to recover the lost tradition. Those engaged in such efforts are not motivated necessarily by a desire to rewrite Western intellectual and cultural history in a different way. They are not necessarily interested either in the Catholic religious and theological controversies of the sixteenth and seventeenth centuries. They are not searching for the roots of ancient dogma. Rather, they wish to take up the age-old spiritual quest anew, and, as in the formative era in Cistercian history, they are working to reestablish a vital harmony between the various levels and components of the self. It is also intended that foreclosed areas of consciousness be opened so that the individual might live in fuller harmony with all that is genuinely supportive.

In outline, therefore, the proposal follows this sequence. The starting point is the apparent ability of Eastern spiritual teachers to assist Westerners to rediscover a fitting correspondence between love and authority. Father Basil and Father Thomas utilize this occurrence to redirect attention to significant Cistercian aspirations typical of the mindset of the twelfth and thirteenth centuries, through which a similar kind of harmony was enunciated. As they see it, the same harmony must be expressed anew. Indeed, it is entirely fitting that the reexpression be guided by respect for the tradition of which the monks of Spencer serve as faithful custodians. In its most explicit expression, the age-old compulsion is responsible for the contemprary revival of the place of spiritual fathers and mothers. The monastic form of mentorship is dependent upon the vitality of the medieval intention.

In this regard it is very significant that all are talking about a distinctively *spiritual* form of fatherhood and motherhood. That is, in Father Basil's view, the young Americans turned to gurus such as the Maharishi because they exhibited human qualities the young people seemed unable to find before. What

Father Basil could have added is that spiritual parenthood became attractive at a time when many were delaying their natural parenthood, which was only partly due to the alarm about overpopulation.

It is instructive to consider, also, that much that has transpired in the West since World War II has tended to focus on a specific generation, namely, those born after the close of the war, with parents who had known the war experience firsthand. It is safe to assume that, in the wake of the traumas of Hiroshima, Nagasaki, and the Holocaust, revised forms of consciousness have come into being precisely from the recognition that the threat of nuclear annihilation is both real and imminent. Those born after 1945 are the first generation of human beings who have to live their lives with this fact as an incontestable condition of existence.

Consequently, President John F. Kennedy's reference to a "new generation of Americans" in his inauguaral address in 1961 is an accurate one. He was speaking on behalf of the children, then entering adolescence, who had been fathered and mothered by World War II veterans. And the subsequent sociopolitical upheavals of the sixties coincide with the coming of age and increasing influence of this particular subgroup within the society.

From this time onward, significant social and cultural events can be correlated with the specific needs and intentions of this group as they pass through stages in their life cycle. The upheavals in the colleges and universities, for example, came at the very moment the same generation achieved majority student representation. The Vietnam War became exceedingly problematic at precisely the time that this group became eligible for the draft. The post-war generation was the one that revolutionized music, created new art forms, found its way into altered states of consciousness—all in clear, resolute, and sometimes dramatic opposition to the debilitating and denaturalizing effects of artificiality and "fabrication." Along the way, they also

discovered the world of Benares, both actually (that is, physi-
cally and geographically) and as a symbol of the wonderfully
liberating teachings of the East. Certainly, such influences
could be found in Western culture before the sixties. But the
large wave didn't come until after World War II, thanks to the
writings of D.T. Suzuki; Alan Watts; the San Francisco poets,
such as Kenneth Rexroth and Alan Ginsberg; and, not least,
Thomas Merton. Significantly, it was primarily the children of
people involved directly in the war who received this spiritual
legacy and who became nurtured by the wisdom of Hindu, Buddhist, and Taoist thought. Then they sought out wise and reliable spiritual masters who had not been tainted by the dominant form of life in the West—teachers who could take them on
interior journeys that their own inherited religion seemed inca-
pable of either outlining or making accessible.

Thus, when we refer to changes in the spiritual climate, we
are not referring to events of a narrowly religious nature. For
the adjustments that have come about since World War II also
affect ways in which parental roles and responsibilities are being interpreted and practiced. Robert Jay Lifton's analyses illustrate that enormous changes have occurred in the ways in
which both mentorship and authority are exercised since the
dawning of the nuclear age.[1] But equally dramatic are the
changes in generational continuity and in conceptions of family
formation. As Landon Y. Jones has illustrated in *Great Expectations: America and the Baby Boom Generation*, the generation born immediately following World War II is having less
than half as many children as their parents. Even when future
projections are taken into account, one of every four women will
remain childless. And those who do bear children have opted for
significantly smaller families.[3] All of this points to fresh appraisals of the processes of procreation and generativity.

As a general rule it seems, it has always been quite natural for
human beings to prepare the world for offspring, that is, to care
for the next generation. Each generation has taken steps to

pass the world on to the next. So natural is this process that every society possesses highly developed rituals through which generational succession takes place; they also utilize mythologies to explain the same.

It seems characteristic of the generation of persons born into the nuclear age to wish to rethink and, perhaps, interrupt or halt the generational process so that it might be reestablished according to more refined sensitivities. Put in another way, the nuclear age has made procreation problematic. Because of the threat of nuclear annihilation, there is a deep lack of confidence in the anticipated future course of humankind. Setting things right involves much more than an effort to correct this or that element, or to take this or that specific step. What is needed is infinitely more radical. If "belief in the species" is to be recovered, it must be reconstituted on new grounds and in new terms. It isn't enough that the cycle be allowed to roll on and on, one generation following the one before. No. Hiroshima, Nagasaki, and the Holocaust, as well as the very real possibility that each might occur again, devastatingly broke the cycle. Since there was this cataclysmic interruption of the usual and normal flow of things, there is now a deliberate intention to gain some firmer control, or, at least, not to lend sanction until the process can be initiated anew. For some, the sentiment is expressed by exercising the option to stand outside the process, to make no permanent contributions whatsoever to the devastation it carries. Others are utilizing the occasion to idealize a new world, to proclaim a new age, or perhaps only a new wave, wherein human potential can be redirected toward more refined goals. Both exhibit the conviction that unless the trajectory is altered, the generative process seems self-contradictory.

Erik Erikson has vividly illustrated that, while the dynamics of this complicated process are being worked out, people wishing to effect generative roles are pulled into periods and states of deep and extensive self-absorption.[4] It would follow, then, that the contemplative or monastic life may be one of the forms, or modes, in which such self-absorption is being lived out. Monastic life, in this sense, may be a form of moratorium.

This helps explain why places like Saint Joseph's Abbey have become very attractive. It is not that the people who visit there wish to become real monks. It is too simplistic to suggest that they are seeking some temporary relief so as to be equipped to go back into the world, ready to face conflict. This is true at times. But the motivation is more complex.

Deep down, there is a strong compulsion to reestablish human experience on some permanent bases, and to commit whatever time is necessary—before time runs out—to allow this to happen. The other side of this is that people wish to feel at home in the world, and not to be destroyed by the artificiality, fabrication, and impermanence. There is a desire to return to the time and place when life's foundations have stable generational grounding. And, given the monastery's position on the edges and margins of society—a participant in the process without being fully implicated, as if it were socially and culturally immaculately conceived—it is being looked to as holding the prospect of a new creation. The deeper intention, of course, is to recapture the promise of having the world whole again.

6

MONT-DE-CATS

In northern France, in the land of Flanders, very near the Belgian border, high atop a large mound that can be seen for miles and miles, stands the Abbey of Mont-de-Cats.

From its walls one has a panoramic view of the countryside: rolling farmland dotted by an assortment of villages. It is as if some giant sower had stood on top the hill and planted dwelling places by scattering seeds by the handful. Each town is clustered around a church spire. For some there are several. Each one points skyward, penetrating soft, lazy, drifting broken clouds being eased eastward by wind off the English Channel.

Dunkirk lies off in the distance to the west and slightly to the north. In glimpsing it from afar, one recalls that it was a frequently embattled city, the place from which British troops were forced to evacuate in 1940, a city that was recaptured in 1945 after being nearly totally destroyed. Smoke from the factories of Calais, also an important city in the history of Western warfare, and now one of Europe's busiest ports, can be viewed in the westerly direction too, a bit further to the south.

There is calm and hush enunciated by the prominence of the monastery. It is instilled by the vivid reminders that thousands of lives have been lost in this area during the wars.

The little roads all around direct travelers to the many cemeteries in the area. All of them are neatly kept, trimmed, and watered. And the bodies in the graves seem to be under permanent military command to remain in official formation. There are other cemeteries too, nonmilitary cemeteries, more than any region's fair share. People continue to live here, of course, but it is even more evident that many have died here. Even in the nonmilitary plots, the graves and gravestones crowd up alongside each other, as if seeking support or solace through close association. Here, there, everywhere, life-size figures of Jesus of Nazareth on the cross watch over the dead.

Today, any day, there are young boys riding bicycles and older ones motorcycles—as their predecessors had done before —on the roads and sidewalks spanning the fields. In the fields themselves, children are playing games. Further on, a family is in the field together, picking flowers, laughing, frolicking, skipping, then kneeling together in a circle to enjoy a picnic meal.

Closer to the monastery, a young couple sits on the grass beneath a tree. One surmises that they have brought their newly found awareness of each other close to the holy place to receive blessing and confirmation. Persons walk by with cameras, chatting excitedly, wishing that the postcards and monks' cheese they have purchased in the shop across the street will sustain the memory of the day.

And, as the scene unfolds, the sun is beginning to move into position over the waters beyond Dunkirk and Calais. Soon day will give way to evening, then evening to night, then night to new day.

This day could have been almost any day, for many of its ingredients will be repeated tomorrow, and the next day, and the next. The story will go on, while some in the cast of characters will be replaced by others. But the majority of characters and roles will remain the same.

I was part of the scene one day, having penetrated from the outside by journeying from Paris to Lille, then to Bailleux, then eight or nine miles to the top of the hill. I came because I had been told by more than one person that the Abbey of Mont-de-Cats is an out-of-the-ordinary monastery, one whose spiritual vitality is recognized by monks the world over as being worthy of profound respect. I arrived at the holy hill with few leads, except some knowledge of the interests of the abbot, Dom Andre Louf, who first came to attention because of his books on spirituality and prayer. "Modern spiritual classics" they have been called. As a consequence, Dom Andre has become well known in the United States, particularly among those who like to keep track of major contemporary influences upon the formation of the contemplative life. I didn't know very much about the abbot or the abbey, but the information and urgings had been forceful and persistent enough to encourage the journey.

Coming such a distance with an intrigue and expectation that grew with every mile, one may be put off a bit by the evident, deliberate, and conspicuous austerity of the place. There were signs in every suitable place announcing that one was approaching private and cloistered property. All doors were locked, of course, and there were no bookstore, cardshop, or knickknack place on the premises to serve as a buffer zone before one stepped onto consecrated territory. It was evident that Mont-de-Cats was not as open to visitors as other Trappist monasteries. Everything about the place told of a communal living environment that was circumspect and formal. This was not a place whose identity shifted with the winds and the tides. Rather, it had served both as beacon and as bastion, a spiritual fortress, in an embattled locale.

I was told by the first monk I met that "it is not possible to visit the monastery." But this, I am certain, was prompted in part by the awkward way in which I introduced myself. I discovered, once again, that being from "Californialand," as Jacob Needleman described it in his book *Sacred Tradition and Present Need*, did not evoke instant admiration, affection, or even very much intrigue. But it was possible, I am told, to sit in the sanctuary during the saying of the daily offices, to worship with the monks. As I was being shown where the church was, I was also directed to notice the location of the door through which one passes as one leaves the monastery.

The church was a beautiful white sanctuary, recently restored according to early normative Cistercian architectural principles. It was designed to exemplify the maxim that structures be kept as simple as possible. The Cistercians follow cherished tradition in this respect. The most famous of them all, Saint Bernard of Clairvaux, set the aesthetic pattern himself. In the twelfth chapter of a book called *Apologia ad Gulielmum sancti Theodorici abbatem*, he placed restrictions on decoration and ornamentation in places of worship on the basis that such excesses obscure a deeper liturgical grounding for spiritual worship. Clearly, the monks at Mont-de-Cats heeded his warning.

Following the liturgy, one of the monks in the community was given an hour of his time to spend with me. He was a bright man, under forty years of age, relatively new to the community, very intent, trying his best to listen carefully and communicate clearly. He told me what he knew and remembered about the war, about the bombing of the beautiful sanctuary during both world wars, the occupation of the troops, the battles that took place on all sides of the hill and in the lands below that looked so peaceful. We looked out from the hill across into Belgium, then in the direction of Dunkirk, then out to the area where Calais lay. Focusing next on the monastery itself, he apologized, to an extent, for the plainness of the monastic buildings, and explained that this style was in keeping with the intention of the monks to live simply. We walked around the grounds, through the gardens, along the walkways. He took me back inside the sanctuary, where we examined the various works of art more carefully. There was a wonderfully poignant twelfth-century sculpture of the Madonna and child, done in the same style as many of the figures inside the Cathedral of Notre Dame in

Paris. There were two paintings of the face of Christ, both superb examples of primitive Flemish art. One showed Christ in triumph, the other in his sufferings. They have been placed back to back, as were corresponding figures on the cross to which they were attached. The "triumph side" was visible to the congregation during all times of the year except Lent, when the face of the suffering Christ was placed more prominently. There were some icons, too, that an abbot from Moscow brought to Mont-de-Cats during a visit. As we walked about, speaking quietly, monks came in and out, some to kneel and pray, others to change hymn numbers, gather the missals together, rearrange the flowers. One of the monks sat at the keyboard of a large baroque pipe organ and played, I surmised, a wonderful organ concerto. I couldn't be sure, for I couldn't hear it. Nor could anyone else. He was listening to his playing through earphones. The rest of us could only infer what melody was being produced.

Outside the chapel area, the conversation became more animated when I asked my host and guide about the abbot. "He is a very strong man" was the initial reply. I commented that Andre Louf's books on prayer figured prominently in the increasing attention being paid to the dynamics of spirituality within the United States. My guide sighed, explaining that the abbot's increasing notoriety had forced him to be away from the monastery more frequently. Indeed, he was away that day, but only on a short journey. He added that he missed him, and that the community sensed and reflected his absence.

This led to discussion about the relation of abbot and community. My host said that the community was a reflection of the abbot's strengths. He suggested that this was a monastic pattern. I was told that Dom Andre's greatest strength was his sensitivity to individual need. He had private counsel with each monk at least once a month. There were immediate and forceful positive responses to both of my following questions. First, does the community regard the abbot as a "spiritual father"? And, second, would the abbot acknowledge the same about himself?

At this point, my host volunteered an autobiographical account. He began to tell me about his own life before he came to the monastery. He had been very far from anything religious, he said, though without considering himself disoriented. But it became increasingly evident to him that the experiments in living in which he was engaged had not provided inner peace, or personal satisfaction. He had moved from place to place. Then, when he visited the monastery and met the abbot, he knew that his "quest for inner peace had found an answer." As he looked back, he recognized that it was the *"radical nature* [emphasis his]" of the answer that became most compelling. It was the combination of austerity and simplicity that beckoned him. Had it been less austere, he wouldn't have perceived it to be an answer. Besides, the monastic form of life gave him something to aspire toward and the means of doing it. Nothing else had combined intense compulsions with such an extraordinary quality of life. Gesturing toward the long reaches of farmland and community life beyond and below us, he observed, "There must be separation from the world, or else how can one find peace?" He went on, though I wasn't arguing with him, "It is impossible to eat of two worlds." Then he reminded me that Saint Paul said, "I have been crucified to the world, and the world has been crucified to me." This was the way it must be. Knowing this, he no longer read newspapers, watched television, or listened to the radio. He did not wish to be diverted to a compromise. For, if he were, his world would become sullied, then would come apart. He assured me that his way of life was the result of a personal decision, reinforced by monastic regulations. He added that he didn't feel completely isolated: sections from some newspapers were read aloud to the community once each week during dinner.

I asked him if many persons came to visit the place, and he said, as I had expected, that the guest house was full on weekends, and the sanctuary overcrowded with people on Sundays. Many drive all the way from Paris to be there. I asked him what he made of this, and he hardly responded at all. Contemporary trends in religion was not a subject in which he placed much importance. He added that the community had made no effort to transmit its meditational techniques or knowledge to anyone outside it. All of this was reported with no visible sign of emotion. It was simply the way it was, and there was no reason to wonder why it should be different.

"What about the younger monks?" I asked. "Is there attraction to Eastern religions? Have the monks incorporated Asian meditational practices?" Before I could finish the question, he had answered, "The West has its own tradition of spiritual teachers." He explained his attitude. The East was a world he did not know. It wasn't his world, it wasn't our world, and he never expected to visit it. It simply wasn't a culture to which he belonged. Hence, there was no need to try to incorporate what insight or wisdom may be lodged there into Western formulae. I gathered that this was too much like trying to eat from two worlds at the same time.

His aloofness disturbed me, and I found his self-assurance unattractive. But this was his home, not mine. And it was becoming increasingly apparent that I had come to the mountaintop with interests and investments that were not clearly perceived there, at least not by him, and, by some prevailing canons of monastic perceptions, were of questionable status. No, I did not come to the place to seek membership in the community, take monastic vows, confess my sins, or pay appropriate tribute. And yet my interest was a personal one, in part, and my journey was prompted by something other than curiosity. Had the interest not been a personal one, I might have been satisfied with mere information: about the history of the institution, the aspects of religious life that are emphasized, monastic aspirations, portrayals of the meaning of religious devotion, and the like. I was searching for the basis of a new rapprochement between the monastery and the world, and I found no leads that I could pursue. Of course, it was not rapprochement that this monastery seemed to wish to effect, but its opposite. The assumption was that there was a spiritual kingdom and an earthly world, and it was necessary to keep the two separated from each other. It would be impossible, as my guide had said, to eat from two distinct worlds.

During the course of my time there, the impression continued to grow that Mont-de-Cats was a monk's monastery. It was a spiritual laboratory for all who lived there, and the venerable abbot functioned as a spiritual father for the entire community. It was in keeping with this sense of purpose that the community sharply distinguished its interpretation of life from those that were rooted outside. I was visitor, and I was observer. The further I probed, the more of a spectator I became. The rites of entry were neither simple to identify nor easy to conform to.

As I drove back down the hill, away from the monastery, I felt both disappointment and relief. My brief encounter had not encouraged me to probe deeper or further. I didn't want to stay longer. Casting about for something familiar, I discovered a half-eaten apple among my belongings. I had been chewing on it, hours before, when I caught sight of the holy mound. I could hardly remember having started it. Now, it tasted exceedingly good to me. I ate it, all the way to the core, with gusto and abandon. I relished each exquisite bite, being unable to imagine how it could have tasted better. And, after finishing eating the apple, I opened the car window to dispose of the small remains, the seeds and a portion of the core.

But, quite suddenly and acutely, I caught myself. I couldn't bring myself to toss these small bits of apple away. It wasn't that I wanted to keep them, nor that I cherished a souvenir. And I wasn't exhibiting an ecological sensitivity either, for I knew that apples are not counted as litter when they are thrown away into grassy or wooded countryside areas.

Plainly and simply, I encountered a strong reluctance to leave anything of myself behind. I wanted the entire scene to exist just as it was before, almost as if I hadn't entered this world at all. I was not only a visitor from some place else. I also felt like an intruder, like I had been trespassing on someone else's holy ground.

My host and guide had been speaking from within the interests and priorities of a world no longer accessible to me, at least not in the form in which it was simultaneously being presented to me and withheld from me. But he wasn't alone in advocating it or in communicating its reality. The entire countryside, the culture and living environment, seemed more and more to be in harmony with it.

By contrast, sharp contrast, I had come from somewhere else, somewhere far outside the boundaries of this territory. This world was not mine, or no longer mine. I felt some nostalgia—and great ambivalence—in acknowledging this. Or, if this world had ever been mine before, it would never be so again. It couldn't enclose me. And I no longer had the energy or the interest to try to make it fit. It seemed more prudent, and, in this sense, more "Cistercian," to leave it alone and leave it intact.

Certainly, I recognized that there was no reason in this world, or any other, why the monks there couldn't do and be what they wanted to do and be. There was no reason either why the people living there should not live the simple way they did, nourished by the fulfillment of fundamental needs. But the world from which I wanted to separate myself was not the one to which this one provided a living alternative.

As I was leaving Mont-de-Cats, I passed the village cemetery. Driving by slowly, I noticed three older persons there tending two graves. One of them, a woman, was kneeling alongside one of the gravestones. I brought the car to a near crawl, wishing both to observe the ritual and to still all machine noise during these acts of veneration and respect. But it became difficult for me to be an observer without also being observed, and I surmised that, were they to catch sight of me as I watched them, doubtless they would stop what they were doing, at least for a while. And if they ever began to do what I was doing, stopping what I was doing to watch them do what they were doing, they might never be able to return to it. I didn't want to be responsible for any cessation of ritual activity, perhaps, because I recognized that my world had no adequate replacement for it.

Then, in the quiet of the late afternoon, in an area where so many gallant persons had fallen, at the base of the holy mountain, where the village people had witnessed, experienced, and suffered so much, I found myself moved by the evident gentility in the face of profound incongruities. All about me was evidence of the extent to which unbridled aspiration and enthusiasm reached. Not far from where I had stopped, a community of men had abandoned everything else to seek together both individual and corporate transcendent selfhoods. They had chosen to do this over the top of a perennial battleground. Through the centuries, the armies had marched across, and countless soldiers had fallen in battle. As they did so, the monks had watched them, honored them, feared them, waiting for the cessation of strife and the advent of peace. Thus, more prominent than the monastery were the cemeteries, both military and civilian.

As I contemplated the scene, it seemed true to me that all of us—the monks, the village people, the soldiers dead in combat, and me, the visitor—were in it together. Each could be regarded, in Isaac Bashevis Singer's phrase, as "victims of our own passions." Yet all of us also aspired to be heroes, too, those who renounce all else to grasp more firmly what they know to be primary and fundamental, those who search for more than that which symmetrical simplicity affords.

The eloquent expression of these aspirations in a place in which death and life were so inextricably and curiously intertwined was nearly too much for me, for I found it to be a place where involvement in the one entailed dependence upon the other, a mound on the earth supported primarily by the soul and blood of would-be heroes and martyrs. Even before the sun had set, I found myself losing grip on which was which.

7

REDWOODS

It can be reached only through a penetration of the dense primeval forest. This involves a journey over rough terrain, through cascading blends of light and dark, in and out of shadows, punctuated by majestic visages and perilous spectacles.

I didn't know if I should try. The road into Whitethorn and beyond it to the place they call Redwoods was known to be treacherous. It was late, and I was already heavily encumbered. It was also the end of summer. I was experiencing the transition. Savoring the last days, I had stopped to gather small pieces of driftwood from amidst the rocks and trees along the coast. Soon it would be another season. I coveted mementos of what had just been.

But the desire to visit the monastery was persistent. I was curious. The information I had intrigued me. And the inclination was strengthened by reports regarding the magnetic personality and charisma of the abbess of Redwoods, Mother Myriam.

So I started out, or up, or away from, or toward wherever it is that one tends to move when penetrating the layers of discovery and heightened self-awareness that lie along such pilgrimage routes. From Garberville, on the road to Shelter Cove on the northern California coast, heading west primarily, through some of the largest stands of redwood trees on the face of the earth.

The road was what I had expected. Narrow. Windy. Steep ascents. Deep descents. Partial asphalt roadbed followed by abrupt drops onto gravel pavement. Up and down. Around. Back and forth. High speed on straight stretches reduced to virtual crawls along narrow passages or over bumpy places. The odometer rising and falling. At times, it was as though I was climbing over steep, rocky terrain. Other times I simply followed a path of least resistance.

I recorded sights along the way. An elongated ranch house in the woods, bounded by a carefully manicured lawn. Next to it, a ramshackle barn transformed into a makeshift dwelling place. A worn out Buick in a driveway. Chickens enjoying a luxurious home. Stray dogs walking the roads, combing the countryside, watching, lurking, patrolling. Hastily assembled roadside antique shops of near swap-meet variety. One-pump self-service gas stations. And dust. Dust everywhere from lack of rainfall. Brilliant overhead sun followed by deep darkness. All around, shadows created by massively trunked superelongated trees. Trees and refracted light.

Finally, Whitethorn appeared. Indistinguishable at first sight. Undifferentiable at second sight. A small place nearly deserted, made dusty from the heat of the season and the lack of recent rain.

Two men, sitting on a sidewalk, propped against a storefront, drinking beer. Barefoot children all around. One wondered if some emigrés from Haight Ashbury, recalling a season not too long ago and a place not so far away, hadn't made a covenant with the first settlers of the area. The scene carried tonalities of the world John Steinbeck wrote about. But this was further north, and two, three, or four generations later. It was its own story.

We drove down the left side of the main street of the town —not that rules of protocol for motorists had been changed, but because two dogs were resting in the middle of the right-hand lane. Their demeanor served notice that they had come to expect their territorial rights to be respected. Newcomers to the scene could invoke no statute to contest the local practice.

Who are these people? How had they gotten here? Why had they come? And why had the monastery been established here? Are all inhabitants of the area being nurtured by the same resources?

And what was I doing here? From where had I come? What had happened along the way to bring me here—a long way from the library of reference works in the Yale University Divinity School Library, even further removed from religious worlds accessible through careful, theological, syllogistic reasoning, and not even close to the feelings evoked by the haunting stainglass blue of that wonderfully mysterious window in the Cathedral of Notre Dame in Paris, or to the memory of vendors selling Italian ice cream in the plaza at Saint Peter's in Rome? Why was I here? And how was I being perceived? For those who watched me, did the trailer signify that I had come to stay? Was this why the townsfolk had examined me furtively? Was this the reason the dogs were wary? Was the entire scene a part of some grand rite of initiation called for by the pilgrimage of which curiosity had encouraged me to become a part?

I continued on through the town slowly, perhaps a mile or two or three further, past a grassy meadow, then around several gentle bends, wondering if directions had been missed or I had gone too far. Then I spotted the sign "REDWOODS MONASTERY." There was a narrower road down the hill, to the right, over a bridge spanning a dry creek bed, beyond which lay the monastery itself.

A second sign warned that the bridge was under repair. Unsafe for automobile passage. I parked the car by the side of the road and proceeded on foot, relieved to have come to a resting place after traveling the entire day. The sun was setting. The presence of the trees seemed even larger now, and more mysterious. Dogs were howling.

I walked through a large meadow flanked by banks of trees,

in the valley between mountainous hills. I identified a small cluster of buildings ahead of me. Seeing no one, but wondering if, by chance, I was being watched in evening's partial light, I approached quietly and cautiously.

The first door I came to opened to the chapel. I stepped inside. No one was there. A single beam of light from the ceiling cast its rays upon a vibrant red rose in a vase on the floor near the altar. Fitting. An exquisite touch. It was the day in the liturgical year devoted to the birth of Mary. The single red rose marked the commemoration.

Now, farther inside the complex of buildings, I rang the bell at the door to the cloistered portion of the monastery. In a brief time I was met by one of the sisters, who stood beautifully erect, moved with obvious swiftness, spoke invitingly with French inflection, like music, gesturing freely. Veronique, she called herself, and I was invited in.

I explained who I was and talked of my interest. She offered me supper—various kinds of vegetables, fruits, fresh bread, soup, milk, and coffee. She made some suggestions as to how I might proceed, but left me to arrange the ingredients according to my taste. I ate quietly.

In a few minutes, I was joined by the woman about whom I had already heard so much, Mother Myriam. Prior to coming to Redwoods, she had been abbess of a large monastery in Belgium. She had left Belgium with Veronique and two other sisters to found this Trappistine center in the new world. "New world" was her choice of words. It signified the opportunity to pursue an innovative set of rubrics, to probe the resources of a tradition in a context pervaded by experimental tendencies. This remote place in northern California had become available through the willingness of the owners of the land to provide a low-cost lease to the community. It had started in the mid-sixties, with but four Belgian sisters, who were strangers in the territory. Then some others joined the community, but not very many. At the time of my visit approximately twelve women

were residing there; some had taken permanent vows. Counter-
balancing this relatively small number of lifelong committed
women is the community's policy of providing opportunities
for visitors and retreatants. The guest list is always full beyond
capacity.

It took little time to get to the point. I talked about how far I
had journeyed that day. We made quick reference to persons we
both knew, monks in other monastic settings, scholars here and
there who were writing about contemplative religion, friends
who had been there before. I told Mother Myriam how I had
come to hear of Redwoods and of her. She asked me questions
about my work. I enjoyed responding. She wondered about the
mood on campus, the interest of students, whether we were successful in teaching religion according to the compulsions we
professed and the criteria we announced. I tried to speak judiciously, wanting to use the time wisely, knowing that it would
be only a short time. Even a long time would be a short time. I
was aware that my memory was being fed, for the experience
would grow into something with many more dimensions than
were apparent to me in that moment.

The conversation took a different turn when Mother Myriam
announced, "We've had a very important day here today."
"Oh?" I responded. "Yes," she continued, "one of the women
came to a point of psychological growth and religious clarification simultaneously." She told me this with effervescence,
moving forward in the chair, wishing to sketch in more of the
details. "What is more, all of the rest of us sensed it." I looked
at her, knowing she hadn't finished, wondering if she would
continue. But she paused, changing her demeanor. Without any
further clarification, she added, "It has caused me to reflect on
the role of Christ—Christ the archetype." She had more to say,
I was sure. But she stopped.

"Tell me," she continued, "does the word *archetype* bother
you?" Then, with some hesitation, Mother Myriam tried to
summarize the effect of the day's event on the life of the com-

munity. It was joyful, enthusiastic, and apparently contagious; but I was given no more information.

We did not continue because someone opened the door to remind the abbess that it was time for the community to gather for worship. It was the hour for vespers, and we were invited to sit in the choir with the sisters and the priest. I accepted, of course, but with fears that I would not be able to keep the silence and honor the quiet for extended periods of time.

But concerns of this nature gave way to a more captivating preoccupation. Everyone seemed to be looking at everyone else. I, too, looked at the women one by one, studying their faces as I had studied the faces of male monks on other occasions. I wanted to remember their faces and their eyes. And in doing so I tried to speculate on what sorts of people they must have been before they came to the monastery. It surprised me that almost all of the eyes caught my eye too. The faces were responsive. The eyes spoke. Each one looked back. They were conveying messages of acceptance to me. I, for my part, began to feel less and less like an outsider looking in. And the faces seemed less and less like visages of contemplative souls. They were faces of individuals, distinct personalities, who had learned to capture their individualities and not hide from the uniqueness of personality.

The next morning I was told that some of the women had been exposed to or were engaged in some form of Jungian analysis. This didn't explain the personality manifestation of the night before, but it did correspond to it. It meshed, too, with Mother Myriam's reference to the coincidence of psychological and religious breakthroughs. It also provided a specific frame of interpretation for her statement about Christ as archetype. I recalled that this query had followed her comment about the collective realization of one sister's combined psychological and religious occurrence.

One cannot help but be intrigued by the ways in which Jungian interpretation and monastic experience are interwoven. It is apparent that the Jungian strain can give distinctiveness to the monastic impulse, and it is also quite probable that the monastic setting stabilizes the psychoanalytic insights by providing an appropriate nurturing environment. All of this is deliberately cultivated at Redwoods. And yet the explanation given us is that Redwoods is not simply a house of spirituality leaning upon Jungian insights and psychological categories. Nor is it a simple matter of the Jungian school's discovering a new and fruitful religious alliance. It is rather that the complementarity has fostered and created something new—a psychoanalytical form of self-awareness whose religious occasion can be clearly identified. But we need to be more specific.

Psychoanalysis began as a method of diagnosis. Its origins are associated with the desire to make abnormalities perceptible and mental illnesses intelligible. From the beginning, it has focused upon mental and emotional behavior that deviate from the norm. Emotional and psychological health is understood to consist of the absence of abnormalities. Hence, the psychoanalyst employs his or her science to restore persons to wholeness.

While pursuing these diagnostic and therapeutic objectives, the method also discloses a wealth of information and insight about the nature of the human psyche and about fundamental human drives and impulses. And Redwoods has been trying to translate this positive transdiagnostic information into new, deeper, and more self-consciously penetrative and resilient ways of expressing religious sensitivity.

Central to this interpretation is the picture of the human being as needing to embark on a journey, or a pilgrimage (in the traditional religious vocabulary) toward personal fulfillment or self-actualization. As the self becomes responsive, it moves through a subterranean world of archetypal components where it encounters a host of mythological personages with respect to whom the drive for self-understanding and self-realization is deeply interdependent. It needs to find itself by embracing, distancing, and distinguishing itself from these personages. Thus, the narrative of the self in process of formation is told in terms of its relationship to the mythological components of the subterranean world, the rudiments of which are also enunciated, and thus confirmed, in the classical mythologies. Such stories, regardless of how they are construed to relate to their Graeco-Roman origins, are treated as manifestations of significant interior occurrences. Hence, psychoanalysis helps describe and interpret the interior path of self-awareness by providing the language, conceptual framework, and analytical means of penetration. And when the mythological renditions are fused with the biblical narratives, and the cultivation of self-consciousness is made interdependent with a growing awareness of the reality of God, the portrayal of the journey of the self (or soul) is given a distinctively Christian rendering.

Thus, through such coalescences, it was appropriate for Mother Myriam to reflect on the role of "Christ the archetype" in referring to the significance of the event that occurred that day. C.G. Jung could make the same interpretive moves, particularly when called upon to explain how religious and psychological modes of self-knowledge could be coordinant. Throughout his writings, one finds descriptions of the interior process that blends biblical language with psychoanalytical terms and categories. The starting point is Jung's definition of religion in the following terms:

> Religion appears to me to be a peculiar attitude of the human mind, which could be formulated in accordance with the original use of the term "religio," that is, a careful consideration and observation of certain dynamic factors, understood to be "powers," spirits, demons, gods, laws, ideas, ideals or whatever name man has given to such factors as he has found in his world powerful, dangerous or helpful enough to be taken into careful consideration, or grand, beautiful and meaningful enough to be devoutly adored and loved.

The consequence of approaching religion from the perspective of being "a doctor and a specialist in nervous and mental dis-eases" is to see religion as being something other than a creed or set of beliefs. "I want to make clear that by the term 'reli-gion' I do not mean a creed." But there is a place for creeds in Jung's view: "Creeds are codified and dogmatized forms of original religious experience. The contents of the experience have become sanctified and usually congealed in a rigid, often elaborate structure." In proceeding in this fashion, Jung was looking for consensus between the truths of anthropology, reli-gion, and psychoanalysis. As he put it: "What I can contribute to the question of religion is derived entirely from my practical experience" (primarily with his patients).[1] And yet such psy-choanalytical findings confirmed the truths about the nature of selfhood that are dogmatized and sanctioned in creeds. Within this interpretation, the Christian religion is approached as being an important avenue to truths about the nature of personhood. These truths also become perceptible when psychoanalytical findings and religious discoveries are combined. The resulting complementarity creates the possibility that spiritual laborato-ries—like Redwoods Monastery—can be instrumental in trans-posing such information into vital self-knowledge.

But there is much more. The important corollary is that trained sensitivity to the living correspondences between these two avenues of truth—the religious and the psychological—provides sure access to the meaning of the mystical writings. Mother Myriam would hold, I am confident, that these writings were composed from the resources of the same sensibility. The assumption is that even if the mystical writers did not have the benefit of psychoanalytical sophistication, their sensitivity to interior occurrences enabled them to come to many of the same insights that psychoanalysis enunciates in more specialized sci-entific terms. And in a number of respects, they go far beyond the range of that which psychological sensitivity, on its own, could see clearly.

The problem, though, is that such an approach can become reductionistic. And Mother Myriam, like everyone else, wants to avoid this. She resists allowing the Jungian structure to provide the final or fundamental explanation. She does not want Redwoods to be a Jungian enclave. She attests simply that these two sources of information about the nature of the self can be brought into lively correspondence, each informing and stabilizing the other. She is quick to add, however, that the journey of the soul cannot reach culmination through psychoanalysis or psychoanalytical self-knowledge. There is a distinctive additional dimension: to explore the world of the psyche is not necessarily to know the world of the spirit. Psychology plays an assisting role along the pathway toward spirituality, but does not exhaust the contents thereof. For the means of entry to the world of the spirit are the gifts of grace, received through prayer, worship, and the sacramental life of the community. It is specifically to this latter dimension that the entire fabric of Trappistine life is designed to be responsive.

It is one thing to view the world this way. It is another to allow this vision to shape one's world, particularly when it is the world of a given monastic community, and especially when that community has come into being under the auspices of a Trappistine monastic way of life.

Thus, predictably, Mother Myriam has a host of critics and detractors. Some regard her as being too progressive. Some say she is too idiosyncratic and exotic. Many believe she has been taken in by the lure of the Jungian world. There are complaints, too, that the environment at Redwoods is too highly charged emotionally. Its character, temperament, and size make the community vulnerable to criticism of a wide variety. And criticism of the community is invariably directed toward the person who is its venerable abbess. This is to be expected, for it is difficult to even think of the community without conceiving it as an extension of the personality of its founder. In most respects,

Redwoods is Mother Myriam's community. In some respects, the community is the corporate and collective extension of her personality and spiritual vitality.

I asked her how she dealt with this, and she talked to me about monastic obedience. She was aware, she said, of the dangers in the approach she had cultivated. And yet the larger fear always was that the fundamental "contemplative impulse" will be violated by the monastic institution that was established to foster it. She said that Merton was always confronting this problem at Gethsemani and finally had to call contemporary monasticism into question, out of respect for a more fundamental monastic impulse. Mother Myriam felt the obligation to do the same.

Her deeper loyalty is to something radically primordial before it is institutionally monastic. For this reason, the uniqueness of Redwoods lies not simply in its being Catholic or Trappistine, and, perhaps, not altogether in the fact that it is Christian. All of these are secondary characteristics. Its power comes from its intention to derive its life from whatever fundamental human impulses are responsible for calling monasticism into being. It is fitting that these intentions would find expression in the midst of the primeval redwood forest of California, just as many other monastic incentives were first enunciated in the desert. The desert encourages austerity. The forest helps one approach reality as being multivalent and infinitely penetrable.

The problem is that Redwoods can hardly allow any portion of this complicated world to remain simply metaphorical or poetic. Other monasteries provide considerably more interpretive latitude in this respect. Hermeneutically speaking, they are less precise, and, consequently, more compliant. At Redwoods everything begs for specific psychodynamic reference. All events that occur, especially those that are most interior, look to the metapsychological narrative structure for reference and interpretation.

Thus Redwoods is something more specialized than a monastery dedicated, say, to a Christian ideal. It is also a pilgrimage station assisting entry into a world that is being addressed in a particular way. And, at the same time, Redwoods wishes to exemplify the very world it aspires to make accessible.

Persons of less keen psychological temperament are welcome, of course, but probably would not apply for citizenship. Not that they couldn't—it is rather that they might not feel at home. For while the psychoanalytic interpretive framework is not a *sine qua non* of the individual and collective way of life, it is not exactly optional either. It is invoked repeatedly to shed light on the events of the day. It is an ingredient in the map by which personal pilgrimages are charted and the religious territory occupied. In a multiplicity of ways, it provides the idiom and ethos to support the proclamation, "Today one of the women came to a point of psychological growth and religious clarification, and we all sensed it."

No matter how one feels about it, Redwoods is a rare architectonic achievement. Through the centuries the Christian religion has frequently tried to make common cause with philosophy, the blending of biblical religion with Aristotelian—or Platonic—philosophy being a dramatic case in point. But the same kinds of syntheses have not occurred as successfully between religion and psychology, at least not with ready orthodox Christian theological sanction. This is the accomplish-ment of Redwoods. In addition, the blending of religious and psychological elements is made practical enough to be lived out, on a day-by-day basis, within the community, in resonance with traditional forms of liturgical worship, biblical interpretation, and monastic spirituality. As a bonus, the composition of these various elements also offers accessibility to the wisdom and practice of Asian spiritual traditions. In bringing all of it together harmoniously and thoughtfully, Redwoods is well ahead of its time.

Critics of the venture must consider that, psychologically speaking, some of the traditional Christian spiritualities are so timeworn that they could hardly make it through the screen of modern analytical scrutiny. When judged by sophisticated psychological standards, the self-knowledge they enunciate is never very confident, and the psychodynamics implicit in the pathways of spiritual direction they counsel are always subject to extensive reinterpretation. Redwoods is not vulnerable in the same ways.

This in itself does not validate the project. But it does emphasize that Redwoods has tried seriously to come to terms with the religious ramifications of certain nineteenth- and twentieth-century breakthroughs in human self-knowledge. And it points to a larger realization, namely, that the contemporary monastic revival, wherever it is present, does disclose a similar blending of elements. At Redwoods the vitality flows from the interpenetration of psychological and religious elements, and the attempt to harmonize both with the fundamental compulsions of the Cistercian life. Other Christian monasteries have been reinvigorated through the influence of Buddhist meditational practices. Still others have been revitalized by rediscoveries of spiritual pathways either lost or neglected, as, for example, when a repristination of the sense of life exemplified by the Desert Fathers becomes mixed with provocative analyses of the influences of urban society. For some the new power has come from fresh awareness of the previously unacknowledged wisdom of Eastern orthodoxies. A still greater excitement might be stimulated by possibilities not yet uncovered, in which distinctive cultural orientations might be conjoined with additional modes of knowledge.

In architectonic terms, there is always the possibility that the ingredients to be synthesized will be too diverse, thus functioning divisively, and reducing the prospect of unity. Yet, if the classic medieval syntheses can serve as examples of how such constructive efforts work, the creative possibilities are influenced and regulated by other factors. They are defined by the traditions to which the communities are responsible, as well as by the canons by which innovation is monitored. They are modulated by the people, their experience, the place (including the land), the setting, the bases upon which community life is ordered, and matters such as mood and temperament. It is for good reason that creative mystical and monastic expressions, from the first, have tended to find expression in specific locales—in the Rhineland, in Flanders, in Spain, for example— where the distinctive ecological support was implicit in the formulations. The same is true of Redwoods. What is developing there is distinctive to the time, the place, the situation, and the collective experience and aspiration of the community. It cannot easily be duplicated elsewhere, for it involves the idiom, ethos, style, and temperament that belong to its place.

Hence, when the event occurred that day, they all knew it, felt it, and interpreted it together. It was an occurrence in which psychological and religious elements were present side by side, and they had been creating the language to acknowledge both simultaneously. The interpretation they provided belonged to the place, the inhabitants, and the mode by which they, all together, were engaging life. It belonged to them collectively and it belonged to each one. They also recognized— their tradition confirms this—that the rose had been selected to record it, and, from time immemorial, the forest had been protecting its sanctity.

8

LAFAYETTE

The Abbey of Our Lady of Guadalupe, near Lafayette, Oregon is a tribute to subtle beauty and unpretentious strength. Its impact is steady and trustworthy, never overwhelming, like the menu one would choose for everyday rather than for the occasional splurge, like clothes one would wear on the job rather than to an inaugural ball. Other monastic centers —the ones that get cited as illustrations in manuals of monastic architecture—strike one as being of the showpiece variety. Lafayette, by contrast, is a working monastery. Its liturgies are correct, but hardly extravagant. Its choral renditions are musically pleasing, but their harmonic patterns are simple, not elegant. Its architecture is tasteful, befitting the environment of the Yamhill River Valley, but not grand or spectacular. And while the intellectual life of the community is competent and self-sustaining, the monks are not under the spell of some dazzling or dominating spiritual teacher. At Lafayette, monastic aspirations are never overstated.

The abbot, Father Bernard, is an urbane man of refined intellectual habits and cultivated esthetic sensitivity, whose formal training is in psychology. The sub-prior, Brother Martin, is of Spanish ancestry. Raised in a Mexican-American neighborhood in San Diego, Martin jogs the roadways in the Oregon hills in the mornings between vigils and matins, and prays at morning liturgy about the issues of El Salvador, Nicaragua, Central America, hunger, poverty, and economic inequality. Brother Mark is the community's talented baker of bread, the dispenser of the nutritional fiber that sustain their physical energies. Brother Peter, the new novice-master, has recently completed graduate work in contemplative studies at Fordham and Yale. Father Timothy, a musician and one of the cantors, writes liturgical melodies, and has acquired an ability to describe the point of personal entry into the attitude of contemplative prayer for those who are unfamiliar or uninitiated. Brother Luke, the venerable guest master, explains that the love and respect individual persons have for one another carry priority over the peculiarities of distinctive doctrinal stances. It bothers Brother Luke that non–Roman Catholics are not yet allowed to participate in the communion at mass. "Most of us are saddened by this," he confides. Brother Dominic, of Afro-American ancestry, was trained in graduate school at UCLA in all aspects of instrumental and vocal music; he lends his multiple talents to the liturgies of the community. The one who writes the checks to pay the monastery's bills is Father Paschal, the procurator. Paschal worked for a time as an attorney before he, as he describes it, took vows and "began working for the monks."

This is the group, some forty or fifty in all. Put them all together and they look pretty much like everyone else. They are short, tall, old, young, stout, slight, large-boned, angular, with a rough-hewn look, with caloused hands. They drive Fords, Chevrolets, Plymouths, and trucks that have been repaired again and again. They have tractors, too, and other sorts of field machinery. They come to chapel, at times, with mud on their shoes, and, quite probably, with dirt under their fingernails. In other uniforms, they could be working for Greyhound, United Airlines, the Saint Louis Cardinals, the U.S. Postal Service, or even Lawrence Welk. One might expect to find people like them working in offices or laboratories, behind desks in the diplomatic corps, behind counters in banks or department stores, behind the bar at Morey's or Hussong's, or behind the wheels of automobiles on the freeways in large cities. And for all one knows, they might even be bookbinders, bread-bakers, fruitcake-makers, and tillers of the soil. Monasticism, for them, represents an agreed-upon means of organizing collective behavior, one which accords priority to certain shared ideals. And, as the visitor experiences their life, talks and worships with the monks, he or she comes to believe that if it makes sense to them, it must indeed make sense. Further, if they can do it—and do it the way they do—so, quite possibly, can anyone else. For they seem like people one would hope to come upon when one is in trouble and needs something more than good advice. In all that they do they make this fact apparent, that they are not pretending to be religious virtuosos or self-styled connoisseurs of the contemplative life.

"The person who is absolutely certain that he belongs here, and can give the most elaborate set of reasons why is probably the least suited, and is having the most difficult time," Paschal, a veteran monk commented. "Yes, if you ask me to tell you what kind of person will make a good monk, I can only answer in general descriptive terms," he elaborated. "It is absolutely necessary, first, that he be a person who is struggling with the vocational question as being something, no matter how hard he tries, he is unable to bring to closure easily. No, he should not come to the monastery after he believes he has resolved the question. He should come here because he desires this environment for his quest."

"And it is important that he has been successful in something else before coming here." Paschal continued. "It just doesn't seem to work if he has failed to reach his goals and comes to us to test the only remaining alternative."

"What, then, do you look for in a prospective candidate?"

"Well, we certainly hope he has had opportunity for some significant friendships with women before he asks to enter here," he commenced. "We want to be sure that he has earned his own living. We want him to know what the monastic vows mean and entail, and this can happen only if he knows he really had some workable alternatives. And, of course, we want someone who is committed to exploring the life of prayer. We ask him to be willing to place this objective at the center of his life."

Then, being practical and pragmatic again, he added, "But, once he arrives here, he will find the life so deliberately boring that he'll be forced to stay for the right reasons. No, we don't allow stamp collecting." he chuckled. "We don't sit around in the evenings smoking our pipes, talking about going fishing, and playing cards." Then laughing, enjoying the imagery, and anticipating the climax of his description, Paschal summarized, "And the last thing in the world the church needs is a retirement home for some eccentric bachelors who get their kicks growing cabbages."

Understandably, the spirituality of the community is as varied as the differences in temperament, experience and interest. Yes, there could be a budding twentieth-century Meister Eckhart in this setting, although such an aspirant would find the effort rather solitary. Or one among them could exemplify some of the inclinations of Saint John of the Cross; the monastic climate at Lafayette would not prohibit this. But the more representative pattern is a more down-to-earth Walter Hilton, Julian of Norwich, *Imitatio Christi*, de Caussade's "sacrament of the present moment" spiritual pathway. The monks at Lafayette would applaud Thomas Merton's criticisms of the fussiness that can overtake domestic life within the monastic enclosure. In like manner, they appear more than willing to abandon rhapsodic flights into the mysterious unknown, preferring the vitality of their shared common life.

This is not to suggest that the religious life that is cultivated at Lafayette is restricted to the spiritually pragmatic. Nor would it be accurate to report that the intellectual life of the monks is rustic. On the contrary, the place is alive with thoughts and expectations concerning the meaning of the *vita contemplativa* in this period of human history and in this part of the world. Hence, when students and faculty come from the colleges, universities and seminaries to visit or for retreat, they are quizzed by some of the monks about ideas they may be considering, books they may be reading, issues they may be debating, and the larger social and cultural trends they are heeding. But all of it is placed in perspective. For while exhibiting interest in the currents of the modern world, the monks have far more confidence in the wisdom that emanates from the life of simplicity and is nurtured by individual and corporate prayer.

Thus, they give the impression of being men who know what they are about, and who have staked all on a kind of gamble or wager. Being so sure that this life points beyond itself to the deepest meaning it can acquire, they can afford to be a bit carefree about their daily performance, should the latter be judged in this-worldly terms. But this, precisely, is the great paradox. For their eagerness to take the present life in good humor—a sure sign that they are waiting for something more—enables them, they believe, to establish priorities in a manner that increases joy now and that sustains an enthusiasm for larger, more expansive human possibilities beyond the grave. It's as if no longer fearing death, they have nothing less than death to fear either. The corollary is that, for them, the monastic way is a self-consistent holistic strategy (which they would resist interpreting in instrumentalist or mechanistic terms) directed toward the achievement of immortality.

As we discussed this issue, one of the monks mentioned that he had been in the hospital recently for exploratory surgery. The doctors suspected the tumor that had been developing somewhere inside of him to be malignant, though this possibility was subsequently ruled out by the surgery. He said it could have been pretty scary. But actually he was getting excited.

"Excited?" I questioned.

"Yes," he answered softly but firmly. "I thought I was going to be there soon."

When he finished saying this, he gave me that look of delight, contentment and expectation that can only be described as an expression of inner joy and peace. His sincerity encouraged me to inquire further, "You really do mean it, don't you? You are looking forward to dying?"

"Oh yes," was the prompt reply.

"Why?"

"Because I can't wait to see it."

"See what?"

"To see what's there. I want to see it as it really is," he said.

This belongs to the monastic attitude. The monk didn't need to take the time to elaborate the viewpoint that the delusions and allurements of the present age prevent one from apprehending and perceiving the world clearly and accurately. He didn't need to repeat the observation from the New Testament that he who gains the whole world may achieve his ambition but at the risk of losing his own soul. None of these statements were mere aphorisms for him. All of them had become something more than attitudes to try to approximate or ideals to emulate or try to live by.

Rather they had become internalized and interiorized. They described the disposition of his soul. They were already inherent and intrinsic features of the way he approached human life. They belonged to that *horizon*, as Michael Novak (following Bernard Lonergan) called it, by which the events of life are registered, narrative sequences ordered, and meanings discovered and prescribed. They enumerated that set of vectors by which he perceived things, made judgments, deciding what, above all, should be honored.

And this is how, in an intellectually intriguing manner, some of the monks at Lafayette are beginning to view the life of Christ. Jesus Christ, by raising the questions "Who do men say that I am?" and "Who do you say that I am?" forced his hearers and would-be devotees to look beyond all that they knew for sure, or thought they did, for insights that would enable them to find a deeper quality of human life for which they had been created. Christ, according to this rendition, is not the answer-man, the person who replies to questions, settles the debate, brings the inquiry to closure. On the contrary, Jesus Christ is the one who forces the larger questions about human life, and who, in so doing with forcefulness, leads his respondents to recognize the shallow quality of the supports on which they have been relying. The interrogation forces the interrogatee to take the step necessary to penetrate through the illusions to some more permanent realm of reality. The journey in this regard may be so dramatic as to require the initiate to flee, to leave all else behind, as the Desert Fathers did when leaving the decaying cities of a crumbling Roman Empire to live in solitariness in the caves, sands and barren wastes of Egypt. No, the monks at Lafayette do not understand the heavily-forested and fecund river valleys of Northwest Oregon to be geographically analogous to the rattlesnake- and scorpion-infested deserts of Egypt, as in Saint Anthony's time. Yet they too are captivated by the writings of the Desert Fathers, particularly as interpreted by Thomas Merton and Henri Nouwen, and they recognize that these monks and hermits enunciated incentives to which they too are committed.

And yet Saint Anthony would probably not have felt at home in Lafayette. The reason is less a matter of style and taste than a matter of intensity. Regardless of how often and sincerely they confess to it, the community at Lafayette has not yet yielded to the apocalyptic mode with the full fervor and emotional abandon of which human beings are capable. It is not that they are hesitant as much as that even in this they are modest and somewhat unpretentious. Instead, the possibility of an apocalyptic outcome to the nature and destiny of humankind serves to underscore the calmness of their self-assurance rather than to stimulate the raging fires of their frenzy. Even this, it seems, they desire to take in stride, that is, in contemplative stride.

"On Wednesdays we have beans and rutabagas," one of the

monks remarked. "Okay, no problem. No big deal. We can live with beans and rutabagas. It's not very exciting, but we don't have to find our excitement in our food."

A younger monk recalled that shortly after he arrived, he found himself having trouble with the monotony of the routine and the constant presence of the other monks. He went to the abbot in a state of near desperation, exclaiming, "Father Bernard, if this keeps up, I think I'll have a nervous breakdown." The abbot listened, but without comment. After a long pause, he said softly, "You have my permission." The monk left the abbot's office, dumbfounded at what had transpired. "I have the abbot's permission to have a nervous breakdown" he repeated to himself as he walked down the hall. But then he no longer feared its occurrence.

The abbot maintained that a certain quality of time was necessary to engage the definitive nuances of the monastic life. His confreres attested that though he was quite capable of it he didn't like to make decisions on the spur of the moment. Accordingly, when asked to portray the nature of the contemplative life, Abbot Bernard described a fireplace scene in which an older man and woman, married for some fifty years, were rocking gently back and forth in their chairs. By this time, they knew each other so well that every little glance, movement, or gesture communicated large worlds to the other. In the beginning of their friendship, when they were just getting to know each other, there was a lot of talking—one of the primary ways of getting to know each other. After all of these years, they needed to talk less. And yet they were in closer harmony—communion, if you will—than they were in the beginning, as they rocked back and forth, in coordinated rhythm, before the fireplace. "So is it in our relationship with God," Abbot Bernard explained. "It's like enjoying someone one has gotten to know over a long period of time, like knowing that one is in the beloved's presence, enjoying this company, feeling the strength and warmth of an enduring relationship."

Consistent with this conception of the contemplative life is the attitude displayed toward events in the world beyond monastic walls. Yes, the monks are interested. They play their part in the day-to-day life of McMinnville County. Though they don't boast or talk about it, the monastery is one of the largest and most consistent suppliers to the Meals-on-Wheels program in the state of Oregon. They regularly contribute toward the care of orphaned children in the Lafayette and McMinnville areas. And whatever monies or goods are left over at the end of the year are given to the poor.

On other levels, the monks' interest in the world persists. One of them confessed to me that he knew himself to be "an incurable and unregenerated romantic," as he put it. He still liked to talk about the women who were an essential part of his life years ago, before he took the vows. He confessed that he continued to find women attractive, enjoyable to spend time with, although his interest in this matter had never been intense enough to threaten his singlemindedness about the monastic vows.

Another one confided that he missed not having his own children. "You're very fortunate to have a nice family," he offered. "I sometimes wonder what that would be like."

One of the monks learned much about life in the outside world by working with the novices, in their initial spiritual formation program. "They are so bright, so responsive, so eager to learn," he continued. "It must be the celibate's dream."

"The celibate's dream?"

"Yes, it's the only way we have of bestowing life," he answered. "It's wonderful to experience when it happens."

As we were talking informally, another monk rushed up to tell the procurator that one of the electric water pumps, in the field, was not working properly. The procurator responded with some monastic equivalents of common expletives, while inviting me to walk along with them to see if the machines could be fixed easily. Once there, he waded into the swampy area around the pump, sinking down beyond his ankles into the mud and water. He opened his tool kit to apply the remedy, mouthing instructions to himself as he proceeded. On the way back to the monastic enclosure, he expounded upon a passage read that day from *The Cloud of Unknowing*. It was as if all of this belonged to one and the same world, the law which makes things discrete becoming more difficult to discern.

As we walked along, talking about the passage from *The Cloud of Unknowing*, another monk came up and asked the procurator for some money. He needed to drive to Portland to pick up a guest of the monastery at the airport and needed to pay to park his car and, perhaps, to buy gas along the way. The procurator complied, finding a ten-dollar bill. The two joked about how and where the monk would spend the change. He assured the procurator that there was nothing to worry about. He had made this trip before. He had always returned to the monastery on time, unscathed, and with change left over. Having satisfied everyone in this regard, he added that if there was time, he would like to visit a friend in the hospital in Portland. But he would be back to the abbey well before time for vespers.

As everyone looked pleased, one of the monks mentioned quietly that he loved to go to the airport, but usually could not wait to get back to the monastery. "The big city is exciting for a while, but I prefer the quiet and serenity of our life here." Another remarked that he first learned to drive in France. American freeways and the fifty-five miles-per-hour speed limit were a challenge for him. He liked to drive to the airport too, but the abbot believed that his driving habits were too much of a shock for the guests who would ride with him.

The conversation went like this until, as if on signal from some interior collective impulse, the monks returned to their individual tasks. They had assembled because of the crisis at the water pump.

I walked away in the direction of the tastefully furnished guest quarters. I passed one of our students who had just had an extended discussion with one of the monks on the subject of Zen meditation practices. He was amazed at the openness that had been displayed and the extent to which the Trappist monk was informed about the teaching and practices of non-Christian religions. We talked for a time about some of the insights that are shared by the major religious traditions. I mentioned that the Benedictine monk Jean Leclercq expected the concord among religions to be expressed first through their common contemplative experience. The student told me that he had always felt the pull towards something substantial and reliable. Today he sensed he had gotten a bit closer.

I entered the room that had been assigned to me and opened the blinds. In the distance was a little lake in the forest, and a monk was sitting on a bench beside it reading, I imagine, from some sacred scripture or spiritual writing. As I watched him and contemplated the situation, the question continued to haunt me: How can something so utterly ordinary, deliberately simple, judiciously unostentatious, carry such persuasive emotional power?

Perhaps the contrast between their way of life and ours is similar to what one would experience were one to travel back in time to the way life was in an earlier century. Perhaps the exposure to monastic life can be likened to a journey to another country or region of the world, to a place that has not been as greatly affected by accelerated social and cultural changes. But at Lafayette one can experience the power of the contrast in our own time, parallel to our culture, simply by stepping into monastic space.

In addition, the idealism of the monks is provocative. Only infrequently does one meet a human being who has followed, without compromise, the vocation he or she believes to be the worthiest. One finds such persons at Lafayette. Indeed, one finds a community of human beings whose every collective action has been pretested, through the centuries, to determine whether it makes its primary goal more accessible.

Kenneth Westhues, in his analysis of the place of religious communities in the modern world, in a book entitled *The Religious Community and the Secular State* (1968) refers to the Trappists as being "uncompromising persons who dreamed the highest dream and dreamed it alone." Westhues explains how this registers religiously:

> To be religious is to attach one's heart to the one highest dream of which man is capable. The goal the religious person sets for his life is the one perfect, all-encompassing goal that would give complete fulfillment and happiness to him who has become a part of it. Because his consciousness is occupied so steadfastly by the dream of what is perfect, the religious person refuses to compromise his attention with the innumerable short-range partial goals which day-to-day life in the world presents.[1]

Philip Garvin, who prepared a television series on "Religious America" in 1974 , made a similar point. Garvin quoted a Cistercian monk as saying:

> I want to love God with my whole heart, with my whole soul, with my whole being and for this I am willing to let all the things of the world go and to simplify my life so that I can gather it together into one simple act of love for God.[2]

The monks at Lafayette would be the first to admit that while they are idealistic, they also know how frequently and fully they fail to live up to their own aspirations. Yet, in being conscious of the need for forgiveness and restitution, they have constant built-in ritual reminders of the commanding aspirations. Understandably, there is something very compelling about a community of persons whose life is dedicated to the realization of some of the highest dreams. When one is put in the midst of it, it is a bit like witnessing scenes from the movie *Chariots of Fire*.

Then, too, the self-consistency of the monastic way of life prepares the visitor for the explanations the monks themselves offer. Father Paschal talked about the excitement of greeting life as a mystery, like a child who is overcome by its wonder and splendor. Father Timothy referred to the rudiments of prayer, and wishes to use this standard (instead of business success, say, or financial achievement) to judge the depth and worth of human life. Brother Peter followed Saint Bernard's counsel that "the human heart was born old and is meant to grow younger." Father Bernard, in summary, understood the search for God to be that one might find him, love him, and be loved by him, more fully. As Saint Augustine put it, "Our hearts were made for thee, and find no rest until they rest in thee."

The monastic way of life invests heavily in symbolism. Its language is full of imagery, analogical and parabolic references, similes, allusions, metaphors, word pictures, and figures of speech. Contemplative literature is enormously rich in this respect. Its imageries are colorful and suggestive. Significantly, when the monks convey what means most to them, they draw upon the imagery of the romantic and lyrical language of sexual love. Dietrich von Hildebrand suggests that marriage imagery is employed to speak of the mystical life because

> marriage is the closest and most intimate of all earthly union, because in it more than any other, one person gives himself to another without reserve; the other as a whole is the object of love as in no other human relationship.[3]

This expresses part of the monastic truth. In addition, through the powers of symbolic transformation, "lover and beloved" and "God and the soul" are allowed to fuse, to become virtually interchangeable. In monastic experience, the vital human romantic energies (denoted by the word "sexuality") are fixed on a "transcendent Other" (as the literature of the tradition sometimes puts it), and in a manner that requires the inmost self to be intensively and dynamically engaged. *Thus, in contemplative experience, the relation of God and the soul is like a marriage; and, in contemplative experience, the relation of God and the soul is indeed marriage.* When the powers of symbolic trans-formation are fitted to the dynamics of the *unio mystica,* the elements of marriage are transubstantiated. And the person so engaged acquires the ability to use the language to speak open-ly and directly—with and without figures of speech—about the relationship in which he or she is held. Monasticism is the for-mal institution through which the dictates of this primary religious impulse are encouraged to shape the total living en-vironment. And celibacy is a condition in which the identity of an individual is formed outside the framework of erotic human interaction. Yet, in other vital emotional and psychological senses, celibate persons are indeed married.

My own ride back from Lafayette to the Portland airport was provided by a farmer—not a monk—who works part of the land belonging to the monastery.

"Are you from California?" he asked as we bounced along in his truck.

"Yes, I am" I answered, though with some hesitation, given his scrutinizing attitude.

"Are you in real estate?" he continued.

"No, I am not. But why do you ask?"

"We get lots of folks from California up here," he replied. "Real estate people. Land speculators. They come in and buy up everything. Then they carve it up into smaller pieces. They sell the pieces and go back to California. Can't take the rainy winters, I guess. Next thing we know we have suburbia. And then it's gone. It's all gone."

"What's gone?"

"Our way of life," he responded quickly, as he waved to the driver of a truck coming from the other direction, "the way of life this neck of the woods supports. And once it's gone," he add-ed somberly, "we can't get it back."

I considered the farmer's observations thoughtfully, but without immediate comment. Looking back through the rear window of the truck to the gentle valley, I remarked that the abbey had nearly passed from view—to acknowledge that the magnetic wheels of the inevitable reentry to a much more familiar world had already begun.

"Yes, we need the monks," he mused softly. "They remind us of how it could be."

9

CONTEMPLATION
AND NARCISSISM

The preceding chapters were devoted to a description of the significance of the contemporary turn to the contemplative life. Recognizing that recent decades have witnessed a contemplative revival, I wish now to assess this development in relation to other significant sociocultural changes. Can the increased interest in contemplative religion be correlated with other significant shifts in mood, temper, and enthusiasm within the society?

Analysts and contemporary cultural historians tend to associate this social shift with an assortment of factors: widespread loss of confidence in programs of collective action, disappointment over the outcome of government-sponsored social programs, increasing impatience with the workings of all forms of institutional bureaucracy, social and cultural exhaustion and malaise. Whatever the reasons are, this shift has led to increasing reliance upon personal resources and a growing preoccupation with the needs of the individual. There are good reasons to think that the rediscovery of the monastic impulse is one of the primary religious ways in which the new posture is being expressed.

Summarizing these observations perceptively, Christopher Lasch has contended that the prevailing mood of our time is a narcissistic one. This is a provocative thesis, particularly when seen within the larger framework of recent sociocultural criticism, which, for our purpose, can be traced back to 1968, that fateful year.

It is significant that it was in 1968 that Theodore Roszak was putting the finishing touches on his influential book *The Making of a Counter Culture*, published in 1969. In his sweeping and perceptive analysis, Roszak speculated on the enormity and radical quality of the changes that were coming about. He felt sure that there would be a "new culture" and believed it would be both a social and a psychic reality:

> What makes the youthful disaffiliation of our time a cultural phenomenon, rather than merely a political movement, is the fact that it strikes beyond ideology to the level of consciousness, seeking to transform our deepest sense of the self, the other, the environment.[1]

The new era, in Roszak's view, would allow the nonintellective capacities of the personality to become the "arbiters of the good, the true, and the beautiful."

At approximately the same time, Charles Reich was making similar pronouncements and proclamations in his book *The Greening of America*. Reich declared that a revolution was in the offing.

> It will not be like revolutions of the past. It will originate with the individual and with culture, and it will change the political structure only in its final act. It will not require violence to succeed, and it cannot be successfully resisted by violence. It is now spreading with amazing rapidity, and already our laws, institutions and social structure are changing in consequence.[2]

Reich was specific about its consequences. Among its products, he said, would be a "higher reason, a more human community, and a new and liberated individual." It would also result in a "new and enduring wholeness and beauty," to be capped by a "renewed relationship of man to himself, to other men, to society, to nature, and to the land." Such utopian expectations belonged to the temper of the late sixties. But, from their very inception, they were challenged and counterbalanced by a contrary set of sensibilities.

Philip Slater was among the first to sound precautionary notes. Analyzing contemporary American life in his book *The Pursuit of Loneliness*, published in 1970, Slater said that something dangerous was on the rise within the society. Ironically, the very developments the advocates of the counterculture were praising were the factors whose emergence Slater found most distressing. He called it "individualism," and he believed it to have assumed such alarming proportions that warnings had to be sounded.

For Slater it was no mean or trivial matter. He believed that the penchant for individualism during the sixties had placed certain fundamental democratic values in jeopardy. He contended that the three basic needs of the society—community, engagement, and dependency—were being "suppressed out of a commitment to individualism." He explained it this way:

> Individualism is rooted in the attempt to deny the reality of human interdependence. One of the major goals of technology in America is to "free" us from the necessity of relating to, submitting to, depending upon, or controlling other people. Unfortunately, the more we have succeeded in doing this, the more we have felt disconnected, bored, lonely, unprotected, unnecessary, and unsafe.

The tendency showed up in many guises, e.g., "free enterprise, self-service, academic freedom, suburbia, permissive gun laws, civil liberties, do-it-yourself, oil-depletion allowances." Slater recognized that these values were widely shared within the nation, so much so that they had something of the status of sacred doctrine.

Then he stated the crux of the matter:

> Criticisms of our society since World War II have almost
> embraced individualism and expressed fears for its demise.
> Most of these critics have failed to see the role of the value
> they embrace so fervently in generating the phenomena
> they so detest.

He hoped someone would see what had happened so that the
threatening trend could be reversed. What he wished for was a
new vigorous sense of the interdependency of human beings,
and an affirmation of the necessity of the collective reality.

> As a way of looking at the world, individualism is extremely
> cumbersome. When things go wrong, we always have to
> waste a lot of valuable time trying to decide whose fault it is,
> since we start with the silly assumption that everyone and
> everything is separate and autonomous.[3]

Hence, the problem with individualism was not that it was im-
moral, but that it was "incorrect." It was incorrect, in Slater's
view, because it was based upon "the absurd assumption that
the individual can be considered separately from the environment of which he or she is a part."

When evaluating Slater's thesis, one must credit its author
for being among the first to call attention to the most recent
"fragmentation of American society." Slater believed that
American culture was fast approaching "the breaking point."
And he was saying this when others were celebrating the arrival
of a new and profoundly liberating cultural era. Slater was exam-
ining the same phenomena, but in a decidedly noncelebratory
frame of mind.

> The most important split in the new culture is that which di-
> vides outward, political change from internal, psychological
> transformation. The first requires confrontation, revolu-
> tionary action, and radical commitment to changing the
> structure of modern industrial society. The second involves

a renunciation of that society in favor of the cultivation of inner experience, psychic balance, or enlightenment.[4]

Slater views it as a split that is not easily overcome.

In 1974, Richard Sennett published *The Fall of Public Man*, in which he decried the fact that "private psychic reality" had usurped the place formerly defined as a "public world stage." He judged society to be regulated more and more by "intimate feeling as a measure of the meaning of reality." Coupled with this tendency was the increasing confidence in "the innate qualities of the self." In this new situation, persons approached the social situation as being "mirrors of the self." In Sennett's view, the new turn of enthusiasms signaled an abandonment of "belief in the public." And he believed that tendencies in this direction had been developing for some time.

> The sharing of impulses rather than the pursuit of common activity began to define a peculiar sense of community at the end of the last century, and is now tied to the localization of community—so that one shares only as far as the mirror of self reflects.[5]

This tendency and the assumptions supporting it raised a large question for Sennett: *"What happens when 'reality' itself is governed by narcissistic norms?"* In response, Sennett offered that narcissism might be as symptomatic and diagnostic of the public neuroses and psychoses of our time as hysteria was for the period in which psychoanalysis was born. Clearly, for Sennett, it was not simply a matter of tracing a significant contemporary social and psychosocial trend. His was an analysis of the ills of capitalism wherein identification of the narcissistic personality was employed as a means of insight and penetration.

From 1970 to 1980, there were significant changes in mood and enthusiasm. To be sure, the emphasis upon Roszak's "nonintellective capacities of the personality" was sustained through the decade. So too was the turn to esthetic modes of sensibility. And just as was promised, much continued to be claimed for "the new and liberated individual," in the words of Charles Reich. Throughout that important decade, one can perceive a continuing attempt to establish a "renewed relationship" of persons to themselves, to other persons, the society, the world, and certainly to the environment.

By 1980, such tendencies received only mixed commendation. Alongside the positive appraisals were growing questions and suspicions. The critique that became most forceful and pointed was Christopher Lasch's *The Culture of Narcissism*.

To make sense of the dominant form of human behavior in an America facing a new era of diminishing expectations, Lasch used the Greek myth about the beautiful boy who fell in love with his own image, then died of unrequited love and was turned into a flower. He portrayed the situation dramatically:

> As the twentieth century approaches its end, the conviction grows that many other things are ending too. Storm warnings, portents, hints of catastrophe haunt our times. The "sense of an ending" which has given shape to so much of twentieth-century literature, now pervades the popular imagination as well. The Nazi holocaust, the threat of nuclear annihilation, the depletion of natural resources, well-founded predictions of ecological disaster have fulfilled poetic prophecy, giving concrete historical substance to the nightmare, or death-wish, the avant-garde artists were the first to express. The question of whether the world will end in fire or in ice, with a bang or a whimper, no longer interests artists alone.

This terrible cacophony is responsible for the following set of responses:

> Impending disaster has become an everyday concern, so commonplace and familiar that nobody any longer gives much thought to how disaster might be averted. People busy themselves instead with survival strategies, measures designed to prolong their lives, or programs guaranteed to ensure good health and peace of mind.[6]

But Lasch reached deeper. Borrowing his suggestions from two highly competent cultural analysts, Frank Kermode and Susan Sontag, he wondered about the nuances of apocalyptic expectations in the contemporary era. Sontag proposed this contrast: in the past such expectations provided "the occasion for a radical disaffiliation from society," whereas in the present time they provoke "an inadequate response," and were received without great agitation. Ringing the change on the religious implications, Lasch extended his portrayal:

> After the political turmoil of the sixties, Americans have re-treated to purely personal preoccupations. Having no hope of improving their lives in any of the ways that matter, people have convinced themselves that what matters is psychic self-improvement: getting in touch with their feelings, eating health food, taking lessons in ballet or belly-dancing, immersing themselves in the wisdom of the East, jogging, learning how to "relate," overcoming the "fear of pleasure."

He continued his interpretation:

> Harmless in themselves, these pursuits, elevated to a program and wrapped in the rhetoric of authenticity and aware-ness, signify a retreat from politics and a repudiation of the recent past.

Furthermore, he believed these tendencies were linked with an increasingly prevalent way of achieving self-identity in both individual and collective terms:

> Indeed, Americans seem to wish to forget not only the sixties, the riots, the new left, the disruptions on college campuses, Vietnam, Watergate, and the Nixon presidency, but their entire collective past, even in the antiseptic form in which it was celebrated during the Bicentennial.[7]

The support for this interpretation was provided, in part, by Peter Marin, whose comment "The world view emerging among us centers solely on the self and has individual survival as its sole good" gave Lasch the summary words that were most appropriate.

Once again, it is apparent that the arrival of a new contemplative religion has much to do with the birth of attitudes Lasch referred to as "the culture of narcissism." Each is marked by a confessional posture, and each finds expression in the first person. Each looks for resolution of conflict in the form of spiritual insight. And each is characterized by an intense preoccupation with the self and its needs. Both appear to jettison the search for the common good in favor of the dictates of personal fulfillment, or so it appears. From this perspective, the revival of the contemplative vision may indeed be construed as the specifically religious version of what Lasch refers to as "the new therapeutic sensibility." Indeed, to the extent that it is nothing more than this, contemplative religion invites the criticism of "privatism" that is also leveled against the narcissistic temper. So closely are the various themes interwoven that there are religious and theological equivalents for the social and cultural tendencies the new narcissism is deemed to replace. Both the new narcissism and the new contemplative religion stand opposed, for example, to the power of the Protestant (or, more specifically, Calvinist) work ethic. Both seek to diminish the exclusive reliance upon the capacities of rationalism.

Significantly, even before the religious implications of *The Culture of Narcissism* could be discerned and traced, another book appeared, composed with very different intentions in mind, but which could almost be interpreted as a confirmation of Lasch's contentions. Peter Berger's *The Heretical Imperative*, also published in 1979, while testing "contemporary possibilities of religious affirmation," called for a return to the religion of individual experience.

The book was derived from the author's efforts to find out why religion has lost favor in the modern world. Berger had written about secularism before, and he drew on these studies when offering this more comprehensive interpretation. This time, however, he encountered a foe more powerful than secularism, a force he identified as "religious and cultural pluralism." "Pluralism" refers to the fact that the individual is confronted by a multiplicity of world views as well as by a wide-ranging assortment of religious traditions and options in the contemporary world.

Given this variety, Berger knew it was necessary to sort matters out and to establish a basis for some meaningful choices. He discerned a link between this need and the function of heresy: in heresy there is the possibility of choices among religious opinions. Berger explained the biblical use of the term:

> In the New Testament, as in the Pauline epistles, the word already has a specifically religious connotation—that of a faction or party within the wider religious community; the rallying principle of such a faction or party is the particular religious opinion that its members have chosen.

Heresy, clearly, belongs to the network of interests implicit within the functions of authority:

> For this notion of heresy to have any meaning at all, there was presupposed the authority of a religious tradition. Only with regard to such an authority could one take a heretical attitude. The heretic denied this authority, refused to accept the tradition *in toto*. Instead, he picked and chose from the contents of the tradition, and from these pickings and choosings constructed his own deviant opinion.

The point is that heresy has always been a religious possibility. Berger wished to make the possibility conscious and deliberate. And this only makes the differences between the more traditional and the contemporary setting for religion more acute:

> . . . the social context of this phenomenon has changed radically with the coming of modernity. In premodern situa-

tions there is a world of religious certainty, occasionally rup-
tured by heretical deviations. By contrast, the modern
situation is a world of religious uncertainty, occasionally
staved off by more or less precarious constructions of religious affirmation.

Put in another way, the contrast between traditional and
modern attitudes is the following:

> For premodern man, heresy is a possibility—usually a rather
> remote one; for modern man, heresy typically becomes a ne-
> cessity. Or, again, modernity creates a new situation in
> which picking and choosing becomes an imperative.[8]

After having made the case for heresy, and thus for the need
for modern man to select a religious option, Berger described
the list of strong possibilities. He perceived the major choices
to lie within three areas. First, there was the religious possibility of *reaffirming the tradition*—a choice Berger identified as
"the deductive possibility." Second, one could make an attempt to bring the tradition up to date, performing the necessary tasks of modernization along the way. Berger called this
updating of tradition "the reductive possibility." The third
possibility was to *trace the tradition back to the actual experiences from which it began.* Berger called this "the inductive
possibility." It was the third of these strong possibilities he
wished to affirm. And it was from the selection of the inductive
possibility that he found his way back to the stance of Friedrich
Schleiermacher, who, in the nineteenth century, construed religion in terms of "feeling," as in "the feeling of absolute dependence." Berger applauded Schleiermacher's contention that
"the essence of religion is neither theoretical knowledge nor
practical activity, but a particular kind of experience."[9] With
Schleiermacher's support, Berger identified this experience as
"an immediate self-consciousness."

It need not concern us here that when Berger looked for positive examples of this within Western culture he paid little or no

heed to the products of monastic culture. We need not pause long either to point out that he treated mysticism in the most guarded fashion possible. Because of his suspicions in both areas, he missed a great opportunity to develop his thesis profoundly. For monastic culture and mystical religion exemplify the roots of the religious experience he sought. The same neglect is apparent in Berger's treatment of Asian religious traditions. Certainly he recognized and tried to respect the fact that persons within the Western world have been attracted to the religious insights of Asian cultures and have also found Asian religious traditions to be meaningful. But, in the end, he could find no deep and abiding rapprochement between Jerusalem and Benares.

Yet, in spite of these oversights and biases, Berger's work is significant for our purpose because it proposes that the challenges of the modern world can be approached via an appreciation of contemporary religious possibilities. Lasch and other sociocultural commentators included religion in the mix. Berger understands the problem to be religious in nature.

What makes the entire discussion the more intriguing is that, while these various statements were being registered—some from historians of culture, others from sociologists and theologians—and while the library of contemplative literature continued to grow in remarkable proportions, Theodore Roszak was busy preparing a new interpretive statement. His intention was to write a book as diagnostic of the needs and ills of American society approaching the 1980s as his *The Making of a Counter Culture* was for the previous period. The new book, *Person/Planet: The Creative Disintegration of Industrial Society*, appeared late in 1979.

Person/Planet exhibited some new themes, but the fundamental point of departure was not altered. In *The Making of a Counter Culture*, Roszak praised the emergence of the individual and the culture that could be created through individual effort. That statement came at a time when the dominant society was being severely threatened. Over a decade later, Roszak took the fragmentation of society not as a sign (à la Slater, Sennett, Lasch, and others) that individualism had gone too far. Rather, he perceived that the process of "the creative disintegration of industrial society" was well under way which made the need for personal authenticity all the more compelling. Hence, *Person/Planet* traced the emergence of "the rights of the person" in modern society, set out suggestions for the contours of the "new culture of the person," and placed personal and individual responsibility within a broader social and cultural framework. The ultimate context, for Roszak, was the planetary or cosmic one. As he put it, *"The needs of the planet are the needs of the person. The rights of the person are the rights of the planet."*[10]

In Roszak's analysis, the linkages between the fragmentation and eventual demise of industrial society and the rise of the contemplative spirit are both clear and direct. His views in this respect are quite radical. The sequence runs as follows: the conditions for our present way of life are being undermined, and thus are vanishing. The evident fragmentation of society spells imminent disintegration. The structure of the present age is "crumbling away." In response, there is a search for an alternative, a contrasting way of life. Roszak finds the following to be imperative:

> We are going to have to rethink some of our most firmly held assumptions about property and privacy, security and success, recognizing that there is simply no livable future for the competitive, self-regarding, high-consumption, middle-class way of life which we have been taught to regard as the culmination of industrial progress. And we are going to have to undertake that reappraisal from the bottom up, expecting no encouragement from leaders and experts who are the chief products and principal beneficiaries of our high industrial compulsions. It will be up to us to begin coming together, talking together, working together. We are going to have to stop keeping our cares and material goods, our troubles

and our talents, our wealth and our psychic wounds to ourselves and begin sharing our lives like mature, convivial animals.[11]

The most attractive alternative, in Roszak's view, was held out by the monastic way of life. Roszak described this way of life as drawing upon a "tradition far older than the anxieties of the industrial metropolis." Indeed, Roszak found himself being drawn to "the monastic paradigm" when he looked about for "human possibilities that existed before history making became the monopoly of industrial cities." Significantly, Roszak's identification of the monastic way of life as a viable living option for larger numbers of persons makes the linkages between prevailing cultural needs and traditional contemplative aspirations both direct and explicit. It is very telling that the recommendations Roszak seemed to cherish most were those he based upon the correspondence he had been carrying on with a friend who was a Trappist monk. For a number of reasons, Roszak believed the monasteries will supply the "most imaginative and popular response to the protracted social crisis" that awaited humankind. He conjectured:

> Before this century is out, I doubt that their experience [i.e., that of the monks] will seem quite so alien to us. For, if there is any hope of saving the rights of the person and planet in the years ahead . . ., we are going to have to find our way back to a comparable sense of mutual aid, a comparable capacity to live reliantly within more local and domestic economies, and comparable appreciation of the wealth that lies in modest means and simplicity of need.[12]

When one examines the entire sweep of sociocultural criticism from 1968 on—from Roszak through Reich, Slater, Sennett, Lasch, and back to Roszak again—one recognizes that questions have been raised but have not been settled. Everyone regards "individualism" as being the crucial issue, but there is no strong agreement as to how it should be evaluated. Some bemoan its occurrence. Others rejoice and hope that its forces will become vigorous. Roszak praises it. But Lasch condemns its overextensions, calling them narcissistic. Everyone, regardless of the specific position he takes, can marshal good arguments. Clearly, then, it does not suffice that one is a good social or cultural analyst. One can vote for or against individualism, but this primarily is a matter of temperament, it seems. It becomes impossible to decide once and for all whether individualism is an evil or a virtue.

On the other hand, when implications for religion are drawn, there is firm agreement on at least one point: contemplative religion tends to flourish under the same sociocultural conditions that encourage individualism. This correlation can be taken a step further. The several analyses show that the two phenomena—individualism and contemplative religion—seem to be strengthened in direct proportion to diminishing confidence in the abilities of the prevailing society, and a deep distrust of the outcome of established social, cultural, and political processes. Conversely, where there is hope and confidence in programs of political action, or in the workings of governmental and other established institutions, the occasion for individualism and contemplative religion is weakened.

Yet, the analyses do not convey enough. Identifying some of the sociocultural conditions that allow contemplative religion to flourish simply does not provide adequate explanation. And one takes enormous interpretative liberties in grouping contemplative religion with narcissism. For on what basis can it be established that being contemplative is being individualistic is being narcissistic? Lasch tends to give it all away when offering this wholesale appraisal of the attitude of contemporary men and women: "Having no hope of improving their lives in any of the ways that matter, people have convinced themselves that what matters is psychic self-improvement."[13] But who stands as the authoritative judge of "what matters"? And how would one respond to Henri Nouwen's observation that, although the contemplative life is indeed introspective and self-reflective, it is "extrospective" too, since it draws one out of oneself in a distinctive way. Certainly, the contemplative stance is intensive and interior. But the literature itself warns one against allowing contemplative practices to be nothing more than exercises in support of the private or interior needs of the self. Merton's observation about the monk's tendency to become absorbed in contemplation, while turning his back on the world, is to the point.

> Perhaps you ask me what right I have to all this peace and tranquility.... I do not have a satisfactory answer.... It is true that when I came to this monastery ... I came in revolt against the meaningless confusion of a life in which there was so much activity, so much movement, so much useless talk, so much superficial and needless stimulation, that I could not remember who I was. But the fact remains that my flight from the world is not a reproach to you who remain in the world, and I have no right to repudiate the world in a purely negative fashion, because if I do my flight will have taken me not to truth and to God but to a private, though doubtless pious, illusion.[14]

Merton concludes that this view of the contemplative life is a gross distortion. Certainly, there is a form of contemplative life that is distinctively private, for example, the eremetical life, or the life practiced by hermits. But this is the exception rather than the rule, and one is counseled to enter into it only after the appropriate disciplines have been acquired. For the most part, the contemplative life was meant to be lived in community. And, as Charles Frachia suggests in his book *Living Together Alone: The New American Monasticism*, one of the most attractive features of the contemplative way of life is that it offers a form of community that seems authentic and durable. Thus, to criticize the monastic life on the basis that private religion ought to be resisted is to simplify the issue. Nevertheless, the linkages between this form of religion and the developments Lasch and the others portray are certainly there, and they deserve to be pondered seriously.

Before coming adequately to terms with the possibility that the revival of contemplative religion may have been carried forward by a sweeping narcissistic spirit, we should take a closer look, once again, at the intrinsic makeup and structure of the Christian religion. It has been suggested repeatedly that Christianity is the product of more than one religious disposition. Down through the centuries, it has tried to keep several religious impulses side by side, even when they have affirmed contrasting and competing principles. The history of Christian thought can be read as an expression of the distinctive coalescenses that can and do occur when a religion seeks meditation between contrary dispositions. The same history exhibits examples of what happens when one or another of these dispositions breaks out on its own, allowing its capacities for singlemindedness to lead it to independence. Indeed, the various combinations of dispositional forces provide the dynamics of the religion in its cultural forms of expression. They are also the primary catalysts in its tendency to change.

To be more specific, George Mendenhall proposed years ago in his provocative book, *Law and Covenant in Israel and the Ancient Near East*, that the Judeo-Christian tradition has been shaped by two fundamental convenant forms, both necessary and appropriate although in tension with each other.[15] He discovered the one form to be juridical in nature and temper, the other a nonstipulative form of agreement. The juridical covenant carries the preamble "I, the Lord your God, am the one who brought you out of the land of Egypt." It proceeds to a promise that is attached to the fulfillment of specific conditions and obligations: "If you hear my voice and obey my commandments, I will be your God and you will be my people." The second form—the nonstipulative one—is expressed in the words of the simple promise "In thy seed shall all the nations of the earth be blessed." In the latter form the emphasis is on birthright rather than law, on generativity rather than command, and on espousal rather than conditions. No requirements are set forth. Nothing is asked of the one who is being made the recipient of the covenant, just as no one is consulted before being born.

It is significant that both covenant forms have been present within Jewish and Christian religions from the beginning. They are frequently enunciated side by side. It has also happened that one of them dominates for a time, to be followed by the other. Some communities, influenced by the traditions, seem to favor one form over the other. And there have been prominent historical figures who switched allegiances from one orientation to the other, then eventually found ways to keep the two in balance. Paul of Tarsus and Martin Luther come to mind. Both discovered that they had been exploited by conditions within stipulative arrangements that they were unable to meet purely, for which there was resolution only in the discovery of the counterorientation. This is further testimony to the fact that religion does indeed require both forms, and that they function to balance and harmonize each other.

It is intriguing, too, that the two covenant forms directly correspond to the two forms of conduct, or modes of address, around which much of the analysis of this book has been constructed. The juridical form stresses obligation; the nonstipulative covenant expresses espousal. The two forms correspond to distinctive but contrasting views of the deity, too. The one, working within the juridical context, conceives of deity as an authority to whom obedience is due and allegiance is owed, and seeks in his rightful justice (and wrath) some sign of mercy too. The other draws upon the analogy of the love between a man and woman, and conceives the relationship between the individual and the deity to be fashioned similarly. It proceeds to entertain the possibility of union, or communion, and often construes this in terms of the mystical interpenetration of persons. Throughout, its symbolism underscores the fundamental harmony between masculine and feminine, male and female, lover and beloved.

Thus, it appears that the religious tradition has been composed out of the interdependent resourcefulness of at least two schematic structures. Because these two are interdependent and yet each is able to express itself in its own terms, the religion itself is marked by an everchanging kaleidoscope of expressional forms. But the larger implication for us is that these intrinsic religious factors—alongside forces of a more distinctively social, political, and cultural nature—are also implicit in the changes in religious enthusiasm that have come to characterize the contemporary era.

More specifically, one can portray the religious situation in the West in the sixties and seventies in the following way: on the one hand, the era witnessed a powerful and eloquent reemergence of the contemplative impulse, right on the heels, it seems, of a previous social action–dominated point of view. On the other hand, the revised contemplative orientation made no claims upon religious superiority. It did not say that its guiding disposition, distinct from the one that counsels direct social and political involvement, is most authentically religious. And yet, regardless of intention, the religion that gained prominence in this period was perceived to include this connotation. With the new wave of religious enthusiasm came significantly increased interest in mysticism and patterns of spiritual development. With the latter came new and increased interest in the monastic attitude.

It is possible to explain this development as a repudiation of a more socially and politically conscious religious stance. If one does so, one can also invoke narcissism as the way of accounting for it. And yet, both explanations are too simple and too facile. For the contemplative orientation—much of it, at least —has tried to maintain the social and political sensitivities of its contrapuntal religious impulse. There is good evidence to suggest that action-oriented Christians came to discover—or rediscover—the *vita contemplativa* while endeavoring to exercise social conscience in more effective ways. The creation of publications like *Sojourners* and *The Other Side*, together with the mix of subjects highlighted in such periodicals as *Christian Century* and *Christianity and Crisis*, are examples in point.

The turn to the contemplative stance seems to represent a compelling desire to uncover a religiously sanctioned, unified perspective on the world. This intepretation can be supported by the sequence of events through which, at least in part, the contemplative alternative has become discernible, i.e., the enormous upheavals of the recent past—the disappointments associated with the Vietnam War, the Watergate episode, the apparent failure or built-in inadequacies of government, the continuing proliferation of problems and issues requiring concentrated attention, and the deep disquietude, which President Jimmy Carter rightly referred to as a "cultural malaise." Certainly, one could explain contemplative religion as one more "survival strategy" alongside those that Lasch and other contemporary commentators have enumerated. But it can just as properly be seen as an attempt to establish a point of departure free of the bondage to the disappointments that have been all too numerous during the same era.

The difference is that the contemplative stance construes the relationship with the world to be fundamentally a matter of espousal rather than an obligation to be met through a series of dutiful acts. And, in this sense, it may offer some recourse—or some measure of hope—to those who have become disillusioned with the problem-solving, project-setting, proposal-writing, instrumentalist approach to the missed richness of reality. Further, the implicit contemplative commitment to the sense of the whole may be providing refreshing contrast to the pervasive atomism—the spirit of isolating fragmentation—that individuals also seem eager to transcend. We call it atomism because it is a viewpoint that each component of the world is a discrete entity, more or less self-contained and self-sufficient, each entity seeking to avoid collisions that might prove harmful or destructive while pursuing alliances, no matter how fleeting (whether in business or romance), which might be beneficial.

Perhaps no one ever deliberately willed that the atomistic posture should reign supreme in the modern world. Nevertheless, this seems to be the prospect humankind faces. The atomistic alternative rushed in—when there was a large vacuum to fill—after the sense of the whole had disintegrated. And, as remarkable and ironic as this thesis might seem at first, the contemplative alternative is being looked to to help effect a new coherence. It is communion, integration, union, and espousal oriented, standing in sharp contrast to the instrumentalist propensities of its counterpart disposition.

From this standpoint, Lasch's portrayal needs to be studied again. The narcissistic imagery describes the self as a discrete entity in a world whose harmony and integration have eroded. Appropriately, within such pervasive fragmentation, each individual is a self-contained unit, disconnected from the others, except for collisions, alliances, and conjunctions. The world is populated by these individual atoms, moving about, self-propelled (as nearly as possible), each one embarked on a strategy designed to insure individual survival.

If this were all, the revival of the monastic attitude could be explained as being symptomatic of humankind's current larger plight. Interest in monastic life would then signal an attempt to withdraw from the atomistic fray via a survival strategy that carries certain religious sanctions. The recovery of the *vita contemplativa* would then be explained as a coping mechanism—a way of dealing with the fragmentation of the world.

But the same data can just as easily be interpreted as an intention to find and mark out a new coherence, that is, as a truly vital alternative to the accelerating atomistic drift of contemporary society.

Of course, the decision on how the tendency should be interpreted cannot be based on perception and analysis alone. The matter depends eventually upon what contemplative religion becomes, or is allowed to be. The outcome will be determined by the vitality of the *vita contemplativa* within a world that faces the most significant challenges humankind has ever had to address. The monastic attitude will be called upon to help create the new environment, to contribute the convictions and insights it cherishes toward the formation of a way that humankind might live in harmony with the dictates of the cosmos and of our own best sense of who we are.

These requests are being heard by persons whose attitudes we have encountered in previous chapters. Basil Pennington and Thomas Keating, of Spencer, recognize that persons are on pilgrimage in quest of a place where the compulsions of the human heart carry as much formative influence as those of any other faculty. Mother Myriam of Redwoods knows firsthand about the need to create space wherein psychological and religious truths about oneself become near equivalents. Paschal Phillips of Lafayette talks of the need for the cultivation or birth of a new understanding of selfhood. And the young diaspora people of Taizé believe indeed that a new world is coming and that significant adjustments in self-knowledge are the creative acts that allow it to happen. Portions of the same world—first perceived from within monastic walls—must have been what Thomas Merton went out to greet on his fateful but necessary journey to Asia. All point to the prospect that the *vita contemplativa* will contribute significantly to the establishment of a new and resilient coherence.

The realization of the aspiration, however, is never guaranteed. After all, the contemplative viewpoint is hard to come by. It demands austerity and singleness of mind. It was never intended to be adopted by everyone. Wherever it rules, it requires some measure of social and political dispassion on the part of its advocates, and this mode of engagement is most difficult of all.

There are dangers, too, that should the monastic attitude try to move from the margins more closely to the center of our common life it will either become destroyed in the process, disintegrate, or lose its distinctive spirit. This tendency will surely be encouraged if "spirituality" is touted as the latest and best remedy for most of the world's ills—the newest item in the long list of problem-solving techniques.

The contemplative impulse is not immune to the same temptations. For, if this spirit is to prevail in the manner we have suggested, it must overcome the intrinsic divisiveness of those very religious traditions with which it becomes associated and through which it is at least partially nurtured. Put more pointedly, unless ways are found to abolish, negate, or diminish the destructive forces that abide close to the heart of religion, the current fragmentation of the world (for which religious zeal and dogmatism must assume large responsibility) will intensify into more frequent and larger crisis proportions. And when self-protective religious enthusiasms are also fanned by nationalistic fervor, whatever harmony and coherence lie within reach, no matter how tentative or fragile, can be nullified in an instant, even by one cataclysmic act.

These are some of the reasons the outcome lies beyond the grasp of clear perception or predictability. One fact is sure, however. The potential of the contemplative spirit cannot be reached simply by encouraging "spirituality" to become more individualized for increasing numbers of persons. Nor will it suffice that the riches of the culture of some previous century— some golden monastic era, perhaps—are transported into the present. And if the Christian contemplative tradition is going to play any meaningful role, its guardians and advocates must learn how to distinguish the religious implications of preferred creeds from what flows from the *vita contemplativa* more essentially and universally. It is the recovery of the latter that will make the difference, in a world for which the process of cultural formation must be guided by the dictates of the future, even in global terms. These are some of the safeguards that will protect the contemplative renaissance from becoming merely narcissistic.

10

JOURNEY TO CITEAUX

Work on this book eventually brought me to Citeaux, the birthplace of the Cistercians, the little town in central France to which Bernard of Clairvaux had traveled, bringing friends and relatives with him, when he became a monk. The town was very quiet on the early Saturday morning of my visit. Birds were chirping, their frolic from the trees to the lawn interrupted by the menacing onrush of a gasoline-powered lawn mower. Inside the monastery church, two monks were kneeling at the altar.

I walked about the place, wishing to absorb its ambiance. I was no longer interested in engaging any of the monks in conversation. The time for this had passed. I had no desire to quiz anyone, to get anyone's interpretation, explanation, or impressions. By now I knew how to find my way. Even before I arrived, I knew where I was.

I walked into the outer garden area, not far from the door to the sanctuary. There in the midst of a grassy knoll was a life-size sculpture of the Madonna. The mother was holding the child in her right arm. There was cherished sweetness in the face of the mother; trust, belonging, and shared innocence in the face of the child. I found nothing overly dramatic about any of this. It didn't elicit the kind of awe one experiences in gothic cathedrals, the feeling of being compelled upward by the ascendent magnetic power of arches and mysterious open space. Nor was it like the recognition of the power, depth, and harmony of the cosmos in which one finds oneself immersed while standing beneath the dome of a Byzantine church. And it wasn't a mountaintop experience either—nothing of northern Montana, Saint Moritz, Aspen, Banff, or Mount Hood. Nor had the scene any of the swirling momentum into which one can easily become drawn when in the company of powerful statespersons and political leaders. There were no signals at all that anything special was occurring or that this was a distinguished space. No placards, guards, fanfares, emblems, or visible power. But the beauty of the simplicity was arresting, chastening, and eloquent—a mother holding a child in a garden encompassed by a gentle breeze on a bright and colorful Saturday morning in France in early September. This was all. Serene, uncomplicated, untroubled, concordant.

I sat there alone for a while, for thirty minutes perhaps, maybe longer, in the company of the fused figures. I wanted to pause, to recollect, and simply to rest. Next on my schedule was a drive to Charles de Gaulle Airport, north of Paris, and, from there, the long flight home. I was acutely aware that my pilgrimage had taken me back to the source of the Cistercian experience, at least as far back as these matters can be reckoned in chronological terms. As I considered where I was, I tried to recall the faces of some of the monks and contemplatives I have known. I allowed my thoughts to carry me to the places I had been—to New Camaldoli, Lafayette, Spencer, Gethsemani, Taizé, and the other monastic centers.

I remembered the respectful bowing before the altars, the monks marching in procession, the glances of the eyes, bells, candlelight, haunting music, esthetic consonance, the inordinate number of bald heads, the careful smiles meant to maintain the proper distance. All at once I began to see all of it together.

As I held these scenes in the foreground of my memory, I visualized other vistas as background—the view from alongside the River Seine in Paris, from beneath the dome in the Jefferson Memorial in Washington, through the window of St. Peter's Church at Lexington Avenue and Fifty-fourth Street in New York City during the noon-hour mass; the pictures I have of the streets of El Salvador and Nicaragua; the panorama of sea and coastal mountains from the rooftop of our home in Santa Barbara. As I moved about, I tried to intersperse these images, allowing each to be first peripheral and then central, wishing each to be interpreted through the dictates of the other, switching them back and forth and around and about in my memory's eye.

As I juxtaposed these various perspectives in my mind, I recalled Ernst Bloch's observation that it is only when one reaches the end of the journey that one learns what the motion was all about. I had come as close to the sources as I could get. I had come by sea and land to the village of Citeaux. I had been brought religiously to the formative power of the presence of our Lady. Wishing to learn more about each, I stood up and walked slowly to the statue. I had come out of somewhere into Cistercianland. But I was still not far enough away from wherever I had come to be able to view monastic alternatives except from the outside looking in. When I realized this, I was intrigued about how the perspective would change if the attitude were reversed. I assumed that I had found Citeaux from out of my own interests and concerns. What if it were the other way around? I had made strong pursuit, as if Citeaux were the object of my journey. What if the truth lay in the possibility that Citeaux is subject and I am object, and it, the more permanent of the two of us, is the basis for judging or assessing me? In short, I wondered how the events that mark the ages would be interpreted if the monastic attitude were regarded as primary and normative, and the rest a mirror image.

Certainly it would be humanly irresponsible to suggest that society should stop trying to address its massive and enormous social issues, and, instead, make bold retreat to the apparent tranquility of some previous era, whether it be twelfth-century Citeaux or post–World War II America. We would be deceiving ourselves were we to think that we could choose to live in some other time, some other place, or some other environment against which the challenges and turmoils of the present age are shielded. Certainly it is not as an alternative to being responsible that one is obedient to the monastic impulse. It is rather, perhaps, a way of addressing those fundamental human concerns in a distinctive, richer, and more compelling way.

But these are not easy matters. For obstacles are placed in the way of an effective engagement of those same human concerns when they are approached only as "issues" and "problems." To be sure, they are problematic. Without question, they beg for resolution and clarification. Yet, when they are seen as nothing more than agenda items on somebody's "to-do" list, they become much less than what they truly are, and, in the process, become all the more elusive. Correspondingly, the treatment they elicit is frequently superficial.

The problem is that, while searching for effective problem-solving techniques, humankind has come to believe that reality can be approached by a careful scanning of problems. Implicit in this conception of things are assumptions about how the world is to be addressed. Problems, it is assumed, are the basic raw material of experience. They are there to be attacked. Hence, the dynamics of warfare are frequently utilized as being the most appropriate language of description and response. Individuals are placed "on attack," in either offensive or defensive postures. We quickly find ourselves involved in a "war on poverty" or a "war against hunger." Even the impetus for conserving energy is elicited on the basis that the challenge is "the moral equivalent of war."

What is too frequently overlooked, however, is that the techniques are of the same texture as the dilemmas they are meant to resolve. Specifically, problem solving contributes to the atomizing of the world even in its attempt to fashion a remedy.

Attention is applied too discretely. And the agent, "on attack," is out of alignment with the world in which he lives and by which his nobler efforts must be fundamentally sustained.

Analogous is the monastic observation that the form of self-understanding that is trying to cope with the modern world is also a product of the modern world. Hence, it is unable to attain effective distance and perspective. It cannot find a resilient vantage point to be able to recognize the world's deeper nature. The individual is given no way to stand back, as it were, to view both the perils and opportunities of the modern world from a standpoint that is not under their total power.

The monastic vision aspires to be a reliable alternative view of the world and a transformative sense of the meaning of human life. It is able to serve this purpose because it has captured a place "outside," from which vantage point it can offer perceptive judgments. One of the most provocative analyses of the function of the monastic impulse is Colin Wilson's book *The Outsider*. It is to Wilson's credit that he recognizes monasticism to be pursuing a clear alternative not only to the prevailing way of life, but also to the attitude that the improvement of the human situation will come about by prescribing remedies or altering circumstances. The sense of life that informs the monastic impulse is of another order, namely, that of "the outsider." The outsider needs to "break the circuit" in order to capture the requisite freedom. And he does so after being provocatively and thoroughly struck, paradoxically, with the utter strangeness of prevailing life and with its unreality. He can be shocked into this attitude, Wilson recounts, by coming face to face with the fact of the world's deep pain. An encounter with those whom Mother Teresa called "the poorest of the world's poor," or exposure to significant human devastation, the sufferings of the homeless or the hungry, or the deep and pervasive fact of illness and misery—all will encourage one to seek a sure and unconditional basis from which to evaluate human life and seek resolution of its inequities. Wilson portrays the outsider as a person who cannot live in the comfortable, insulated world, merely accepting what he sees and touches as being substantial and dependable. The outsider sees too clearly, feels too deeply, and is obliged, with fear and trembling, to work out his own salvation (and, to a certain extent, the world's as well) in some other terms. He is forced to go away, to retreat, to find a new place, to locate an abode somewhere beyond unreality's control or jurisdiction. Wilson quotes the Russian spiritual writer, Gurdjieff:

> Man is attached to everything in his life; attached to his imagination, attached to his stupidity, attached even to his suffering—possibly to his suffering more than anything else. He must free himself from attachment. Attachment to things, identification with things keeps alive a thousand "I's" in a man. These "I's" must die in order that the big I may be born. But how can they be made to die? It is at this point that the possibility of awakening comes to the rescue. To awaken means to realize one's nothingness, that is, to realize one's complete and absolute happiness . . . . So long as a man is not horrified at himself, he knows nothing about himself.[1]

But Wilson isn't speaking only of Gurdjieff, and he isn't referring only to persons well known in the religious sphere, such as Saint John of the Cross and the other clear examples of "holy men" or spiritual masters. He is also talking about writers such as Blake, Hesse, Hölderlin, Sartre, Joyce, Kierkegaard, Dostoevski, Tolstoy, and a host of others. For the compulsion to become an outsider is reflected not only within the field of religious sensitivity, but it also stands behind the creative self-expressions of persons whose work belongs more comprehensively to other fields. As Wilson says:

> The greatest heights of self-expression—in poetry, music, painting—are achieved by men who are supremely alone. And it is for this reason that the idea of the beatific vision is easier for the artist to grasp than for anyone else. He has

only to imagine his moment of "greatest aloneness" intensified to a point where it would fill up his life and make all
other relations impossible and unnecessary. They never are,
of course, for the artist; his moments of highest inspiration
leave him glad enough to get back to people, but at least he
knows something of that complete independence of other
human beings the theoretical existence of which most people prefer to doubt.[2]

In his own way, Thomas Merton gave support to this view by
describing the work of the monk in the following way:

> Can I tell you that I have found answers to the questions
> that torment the man of our time? I do not know if I have
> found answers. When I first became a monk, yes, I was more
> sure of "answers" But as I grow old in the monastic life and
> advance further into solitude, I become aware that I have
> only begun to seek the questions. And what are the ques-
> tions? Can man make sense out of his existence? Can man
> honestly give his life meaning merely by adopting a certain
> set of explanations which pretend to tell him why the world
> began and where it will end, why there is evil and what is
> necessary for the good life?

And now the key lines:

> My brother, perhaps in my solitude I have become as it were
> an explorer for you, a searcher in realms which you are not
> able to visit—except perhaps in the company of your psychi-
> atrist. I have been summoned to explore a desert area of
> man's heart in which explanations no longer suffice, and in
> which one learns that only experience counts. An arid,
> rocky, dark land of the soul, sometimes illuminated by
> strange fires which men fear and peopled by spectres which
> men studiously avoid except in their nightmares. And in
> this area I have learned that one cannot truly know hope un-
> less he has found out how like despair hope is.[3]

Further interpretative suggestions along these lines have
been developed by Kenneth Westhues in his book *Society's
Shadow: Studies in the Sociology of Countercultures*. West-

hues illustrates that the development of a counterculture always involves a voluntary departure from the dominant society in quest of a living situation that is understood to be more in keeping with a preferred sense of the nature of reality.

> It is an entirely new and different reality that members of a counterculture bear in their minds and seek to embody in social islands that exist in the midst of the rationality of the dominant order. Such a reality is so divergent from our own that it cannot be adequately understood from outside itself, but only from within.[4]

Westhues proceeds to list several characteristics of a counterculture, i.e., that economic communism tends to prevail; patterns of sexual relationship deviate from nuclear family and monogamous marriage norms; little effort is made to impose the life of the counterculture upon dominant society, and direct political involvement is usually not sought; members of the counterculture reject many of the rewards and status symbols of the dominant society, while looking to spiritual leaders who embody the ideals they hold; hence, the counterculture develops distinctive folkways and mores, in isolation from those that characterize the life of the dominant society. It is obvious that all of these features are descriptive of monastic culture as well.

Like Wilson, Westhues emphasizes the contrast. He notes that "countercultures arise in those sectors of a society where day-to-day experience substantially contradicts or insufficiently reinforces the society's ideology." This implies that those who pursue countercultural alternatives must first come to view themselves as potential outsiders of the parent society. The counterculture is formed through recognition that the perceived discrepancies cannot be resolved by political action or the normal means of social change within the dominant social order. In some respects, Westhues's summary statement may seem a bit extreme:

A counterculture is basically an idea; it is something that happens in people's heads. A counterculture comes into existence when a group of people emancipate their thinking from the ideology of their society and come to believe with utter finality that everything they have been taught to be true is in fact false. A counterculture is born when people suddenly discover that they no longer can speak society's language, nor comprehend its logic, nor be governed by its norms. The origin of a counterculture lies in an ineffable moment of freedom from all the sham and hypocrisy of society, a moment in which a new reality is discovered, *the absolute reality*. Monasticism was born out of the experience of freedom from the world of third-and fourth-century Rome.[5]

Yet, clearly and explicitly, the statement is intended to help explain the rise of a monastic movement within a culture, and, more specifically, the development of Christian monasticism within Western culture.

Characteristically, in analyses of this kind, attention is directed toward the dynamics of "the journey out." Westhues illustrates this analytical tendency in explaining that the monastic impulse is borne on the wings of an awareness that prevailing life ways are losing credibility. But the corresponding motion is important too, that is, what John Dunne calls the "journey back into the human circle," particularly for those who only intend to be temporary or "weekend monks." Not everyone returns, of course, nor is there a necessity that each should. But even those who intend to do not always find the way easy. The process is just as intricate for the journey back as it is for the journey out. Neither is mechanical. Neither happens accidentally. Each involves a pilgimage strategy and invokes distinctive rites of passage.

John Ruysbroeck, the fourteenth-century Flemish mystical writer, referred repeatedly to the process by which "one becomes seeing." He followed this with a statement about "one's becoming the light by which one sees." The same insight, it seems, can be applied to the process by which the journey back is effected. But it is an enormously complicated subject, and we must approach it step by step.

I have suggested, some pages back, that problem solving lacks sufficiency because it is virtually parasitical upon that which it proposes to resolve. What seems needed is a perspective or standpoint free of this entanglement. The contemplative alternative qualifies because it is its nature to be conceived in contrast to a prevailing perspective. It is not bound by the same conditions. It provides some movement out and away from those restrictions. It functions by means of the powers of the mirror contrast.

Of course, it is necessary that such a vantage point be discovered, and this is no small undertaking. Its powers and presence are not obvious. Further, even if they were, one cannot simply will them into being. And, even knowing about them doesn't guarantee that one will find them or know what to do if and when one does.

One needs to become released from the pervasive and sometimes nearly overwhelming complexities of the more prevalent orientation so that one can identify the conditions of the contrast objectively. One needs to be able to see from a position that does not lie under the control of the prevailing orientation. In short, one must find his or her place, or mark out the pathway of "the outsider." The process of locating this vantage point may indeed involve one in "a journey to Citeaux," as it were—some deliberate extrication from accepted ways of life for a sufficient period of time, so that the new or fresh alternative can come more sharply into view. One cannot stay in the same place and remain the same person and expect to reach a destination of this sort. The journey involves a departure from all that is familiar and accepted, and an initiation into that which confronts one as being unknown and even alien.

Once on the journey, one experiences other things happening. Little by little, the vantage point comes into closer view. The place at first unknown and alien is claimed as the position from which all of life can be perceived afresh. And then, too, little by little, the vantage point becomes more than a place, position, or perspective. It is also a set of compulsions, a network of insights, and a force through which the original situation is both assessed and addressed. In the process, the newly acquired perspective becomes part of the substance of that which it illumines and informs. For, when it is seen afresh, it is also formed afresh. "Reality becomes seeing," as the world is shaped to the light through which it is revisioned.

This is a mystical insight, but we are doing more than citing a pious platitude. For it seems that this kind of reconstructive process is always under way and provides content for the dynamics of cultural formation. Many of the most significant changes in the modern world, for instance, have come about through dynamics of this kind. I am referring to the power of the convictions of the counterculture. First, these convictions seemed to serve large portions of the dominant society as a contrasting mirror image, and were approached by the majority point of view as being decidedly alien. Little by little, the same insights and perspectives, though never all at once and never uncritically, became the source of tremendous reconstructive and re-creative inspiration. Sometimes dramatically and sometimes more quietly, they altered virtually every aspect of the prevalent society's established way of life. The same attitudinal and sociocultural transactions have occurred as a result of the dominant society's acknowledged dependence upon the perspectives on life shaped by the experiences of minority persons—perspectives that also functioned first as contrasting mirror images. Again, in seeking to come to terms with the contrast, majority society found itself, even while continuing forcefully to resist, being shaped more and more by the sensibilities through which it was also being perceived and criticized.

Such transactions and transformations occur within a society when counter or contrasting positions have gathered sufficient resourcefulness to offer alternatives to the conditions upon which the majority viewpoint is dependent. But they are also called into play in the clash between contrasting ways of life and views of the world. The trauma of the involvement of the United States in the Vietnam War, particularly in the way in which "Asia" became implicated in the emotional and psychological struggle, called the same dynamics into play. So too, the inability of Americans satisfactorily to come to terms with the happenings and machinations within countries belonging to the Arab world, and thus informed by Islamic attitudes and convictions, is another case in point. Arab doings seem inexplicable because they don't conform to the actions and habits the prevailing viewpoint can sanction. To the extent that the alien attitude can become the vantage point through which we identify our own ways of administering sanction, the same attitude can stimulate the prospects for both mutual understanding and peace. But what was perceived first as being alien must shed light, more and more, on what humankind is. Not only do we learn just who we are when perceiving ourselves in mirror contrast, but we are also shaped by the contrast, whether to closer approximation, more radical and deliberate difference, or to something beyond either's grasp.

The process of self-discovery we have just outlined is characteristic, too, of the function of monastic culture. But monasticism may be equipped to serve more effectively than many or most of the other contrasting attitudes because it has grown up alongside the prevailing society over centuries of time. It has been interacting with the viewpoint of the more dominant society for as long as that society has been in existence. Indeed, it has served as mirror contrast for the series of social patterns that have marked the history of Western civilization. Thus, the interest it evokes today must signal that persons within the more dominant society are looking into the mirror, studying the contrast, so as to come to terms with their own society and, of course, to be better able to live. And we do not yet know enough about the extent to which such contrasts remain necessary to the retention—or recreation—of a belief in God within the society.

It is possible, therefore, that we are witnessing just the beginnings of a process that will come into greater influence. We have identified some of the early products of the turn to the monastic attitude. But what seems destined to follow is the use of the monastic alternative as an avenue toward greater cross-cultural understanding. Exposure to monasticism seems to motivate people to think about alternative ways of life, particularly those available within other cultures. It also seems to prompt them to become travelers and pilgrims to other lands. And the monks themselves are currently involved in some highly sophisticated attempts to come to terms with the life ways of other cultures and religious traditions.

Hence it is to be expected that someone like Thomas Merton would have some idea of what he was looking for when he traveled from the Occident to the Orient. He knew what he was looking for, and he was carrying a great deal with him. What he came to look for he had already identified from within the experience of solitariness in his hermitage in the hills of Kentucky. His posture was not unlike that of those persons described in Plato's account of "the myth of the cave," who desire to penetrate to a deeper reality, in Merton's case, through the medium of another culture. This is in keeping with the sensibility that characterize the monastic impulse. It tries steadfastly to hold at least two orientations together, the one it seeks and that against which it stands in contrast. Thus it is constantly creating through the powers of a reflexive imagination—standing appositionally to a world it also cherishes, and taking responsibility for both dispositions.

One should keep all of this in mind when judging the apparent irrelevance and/or impracticality of the monastic attitude. Judgments against monasticism often have vested assumptions about utility, and frequently these imply that relevance is a virtue that entails immediate, direct, and concrete actional responses. Appropriately, the problem-solving mentality tries to identify the techniques that bring relevance about. The monastic attitude, in contrast, is motivated by other priorities. Because mirror imagery is always called into play, it resists the method of direct application and is not compelled by the dictates of literal-mindedness. It attests, instead, that immediacy is not the only mode through which conflict resolution occurs, and conflict resolution is not the only avenue of progress. What is essential is that the contrast be maintained, so that alternatives are available, so that the dynamic interaction that lies at the heart of the process of cultural construction and transmission will continue to be creative and resourceful. Seen in this light, the positive fate of the world may indeed depend upon monks living as monks, not in their adapting monastic sensibilities to more specific goals, but in being just what they are, doing just what they do, sustaining the monastic attitude simply because of what it is.

I came to appreciate this more and more in my journey to find Citeaux. In finding Citeaux, I learned to honor the contrast, and to hold to it fast, until the image and the reality reflected therein become the selfsame unity. We cannot live under the presumption that such unification and cohesion have already been effected; yet we must live in the hope that this shall occur one day. In another sense, the unity and coherence are already deeply and pervasively there, and need only to be discerned, enunciated, and celebrated.

The dynamic interplay between these two modes effects the translation of the world into the contrasting light by which it is perceived. As startling as it may seem, it is by the same contrasting light, for centuries, that our collective life has been nurtured. And the monastic impulse has provided the voice to enable us to welcome it as being sacred.

NOTES

CHAPTER ONE

1. William Irwin Thompson, *At the Edge of History* (New York: Harper and Row, 1971). I have described this visit in *Hope Against Hope: Moltmann to Merton in One Theological Decade* (Philadelphia: Fortress Press, 1976), chapter four, "The Dynamics of Positive Disengagement."

2. Erik H. Erikson, *Identity: Youth and Crisis* (New York: W.W. Norton, 1968), p. 138.

3. Ernesto Cardenal, *To Live is to Love*, trans. Kurt Reinhardt (New York: Doubleday, 1974), pp. 153, 154, 155-56.

4. James Hillman, *Insearch: Psychology and Religion* (New York: Charles Scribner's Sons, 1967), pp. 101-2.

5. Saint Augustine, *The Confessions*, Book X, chapter six, as included in Walter H. Capps and Wendy M. Wright, eds., *Silent Fire: An Invitation to Western Mysticism* (San Francisco: Harper and Row, 1978), pp. 32-33.

CHAPTER TWO

1. Peter Tauber, *The Last Best Hope* (New York: Harcourt Brace Jovanovich, 1977), p. 456.

2. Thomas Merton, *The Asian Journal of Thomas Merton*, ed. Naomi Burton, Brother Patrick Hart, and James Laughlin (New York: New Directions, 1973), pp. 4, 5.

3. Cf. Erik H. Erikson, *Young Man Luther: A Study in Psychoanalysis and History* (New York: W.W. Norton, 1958); and *Gandhi's Truth* (New York: W.W. Norton, 1969), especially pp. 265-66.

4. E.F. Schumacher, *Small Is Beautiful: Economics as if People Mattered* (New York: Harper and Row, 1973).

5. Stephen Graubard, Introduction to "Discoveries and Interpretations: Studies in Contemporary Scholarship," *Daedalus*, Summer 1977, pp. xv-xvi.

6. Henry J. Aaron, *Politics and the Professors: The Great Society in Perspective* (Washington: The Brookings Institution, 1978), p. 159.

7. George W. Pierson, "The University and American Society," in Michael Mooney and Florian Stuber, eds., *Small Comforts for Hard Times: Humanists on Public Policy* (New York: Columbia University Press, 1977), p. 264.

162 • *The Monastic Impulse*

8. John W. Gardner, *Morale* (New York: W.W. Norton, 1978), p. 13.
9. William de Bary, "The University, Society, and the Critical Temper," in Mooney and Stuber, eds., *Small Comfort for Hard Times*, p. 280.
10. Christopher Lasch, *The Culture of Narcissism: American Life in an Age of Diminishing Expectations* (New York: W.W. Norton, 1978), p. 4.

CHAPTER THREE
1. Thomas Merton, transcript statement from Center for the Study of Democratic Institutions conference, Santa Barbara, California, October 3, 1968.
2. Merton, *Asian Journal*, pp. 233, 235-36.
3. Thomas Merton, *The Seven Storey Mountain* (New York: Harcourt, Brace and World, 1948), pp. 111-12.

CHAPTER FOUR
1. Rex Brico, *Taizé. Brother Roger and His Community* (London and Cleveland: Collins, 1978), pp. 13-14.
2. Brother Roger, *Struggle and Contemplation* (New York: Seabury Press, 1974), p. 17.
3. Brother Roger, *A Life We Never Dared Hope For: Journal 1972-1974* (London and Cleveland: Collins, 1979), p. 36.
4. Brother Roger, *Today*, unpublished manuscript.
5. *The Rule of Taizé* (Taizé-Communauté: Les Presses de Taizé, 1968), pp. 11-13, 15-21.
6. Brother Roger, *Festival* (Taizé-Communauté: Les Presses de Taizé, 1973), pp. 27-28.
7. Brico, *Taizé*, p. 30.
8. Ibid., pp. 36-37.
9. Brother Roger, *A Life We Never Dared Hope For*, p. 42.
10. E. Delaruelle, "The Crusading Idea in Cluniac Literature of the Twelfth Century," in Noreen Hunt, ed., *Cluniac Monasticism in the Central Middle Ages* (London: Macmillan, 1971), pp. 210-11.

CHAPTER FIVE
1. Basil Pennington, *Daily We Touch Him* (New York: Doubleday, 1977); and *Centering Prayer: Renewing an Ancient Christian Prayer Form* (New York: Doubleday, 1980).
2. Robert Jay Lifton, *Boundaries: Psychological Man in Revolution* (New York: Random House, 1970).
3. Landon Y. Jones, *Great Expectations: America and the Baby Boom Generation* (New York: Ballantine, 1981).
4. Erik H. Erikson, *Identity and the Life Cycle* (New York: International Universities Press, 1959).

CHAPTER SEVEN
1. Carl Gustav Jung, *Psychology and Religion* (New Haven: Yale University Press, 1938), pp. 6-8.

CHAPTER EIGHT
1. Kenneth Westhues, *The Religious Community and the Secular State* (Philadelphia: Lippincott, 1968), pp. 24, 48.
2. Philip Garvin and Julia Welch, *Religious America* (New York: McGraw-Hill, 1974), p. 55.
3. Dietrich von Hildebrand, *Marriage* (New York: Longmans, Green, 1959), p. 2.

CHAPTER NINE
1. Theodore Roszak, *The Making of a Counter Culture: Reflections on the Technocratic Society and Its Youthful Opposition* (Garden City: Doubleday, 1969).
2. Charles A. Reich, *The Greening of America* (New York: Random House, 1970), p. 1.
3. Philip Slater, *The Pursuit of Loneliness: American Culture at the Breaking Point* (Boston: Beacon Press, 1970), pp. 34–35.
4. Ibid., p. 124.
5. Richard Sennett, *The Fall of Public Man* (New York: Random House, 1974), p. 326.
6. Lasch, *The Culture of Narcissism*, pp. 3–4.
7. Ibid., pp. 4–5.
8. Peter L. Berger, *The Heretical Imperative: Contemporary Possibilities of Religious Affirmation* (Garden City, New York: Doubleday, 1979), pp. 27–28.
9. Ibid., p. 132.
10. Theodore Roszak, *Person/Planet: The Creative Disintegration of Industrial Society* (Garden City, New York: Doubleday, 1979).
11. Ibid., p. 287.
12. Ibid.
13. Lasch, *The Culture of Narcissism*, p. 4.
14. Thomas Merton, "A Letter on the Contemplative Life," in *The Monastic Journey*, ed. Brother Patrick Hart (Garden City, New York: Doubleday, 1978), p. 220.
15. George E. Mendenhall, *Law and Covenant in Israel and the Ancient Near East* (Pittsburgh: The Biblical Colloquium, 1955).

CHAPTER TEN
1. George Gurdjieff, *All and Everything* (London: Routledge and Kegan Paul, 1950), p. 1183.
2. Colin Wilson, *The Outsider* (London: Pan Books, 1978), p. 226.
3. "A Letter on the Contemplative Life," in *The Monastic Journey*, ed. Brother Patrick Hart, pp. 220–21.
4. Kenneth Westhues, *Society's Shadow: Studies in the Sociology of Countercultures* (New York: McGraw-Hill, 1972), p. 23.
5. Ibid., p. 40.